BAD BOY
FROM
JAMAICA

BAD BOY

FROM

JAMAICA

THE GARNETT MYRIE STORY

Basil Waine Kong, Ph.D., JD

Library of Congress Control Number:		2014907845
ISBN:	Hardcover	978-1-4990-1039-8
	Softcover	978-1-4990-1041-1
	eBook	978-1-4990-1038-1

Rev. date: 05/13/2014

To order additional copies of this book, contact:
Xlibris LLC
1-888-795-4274
www.Xlibris.com
Orders@Xlibris.com
550115

CONTENTS

DEDICATION

While this book is dedicated to the kind and generous people of Woodlands District (St. Elizabeth, Jamaica), I am grateful to my support network. First to my wife (Stephanie), my children (Jillian Kong-Sivert, Freddie Kong, Melanie Kong-Shaw, and Aleron Kong), my grandchildren (Mackenzie, Brooks, Audrey, Vincent, Kai, and Hallie), and my brother Earl Kong was particularly helpful in reminding me about specific events in which we participated.

I am thinking of my children and all who come after me as I record these memories as a legacy. I hope my life experience enriches their lives as well. My belief is that culture, relationships, experience, education, and upbringing is like a field with both flowers and weeds growing in the same rich soil. While you can choose to water and nourish the weeds and weed the flowers, our challenge is to continuously forsake the weeds and fertilize the flowers. With a nod to our background, if we pursue education, enlightenment and character, our lives will be beautiful bouquets that will enrich the lives of everyone around us. We need to constantly remind ourselves that flowers will not refuse to bloom because of the few inevitable weeds invade our flower beds.

Our culture is our light as well as our mirror. If you fill your life with good things, good experiences will manifest themselves. I try to seduce and entertain all my senses each day. So I see great works of art produced by God in the form of a sunset, a rainfall, or a rainbow; see man's great achievements in our architecture, language, and innovations; smell the fragrances of flowers; feel the textures of everything about me including my wife's embrace; listen to a variety of music and the voices of my children, grandchildren and friends; enjoy interesting foods and spirits; and use my sixth sense to wonder, to contemplate, to think deeply about what is possible. My grandmother's constant refrain was: "Work as if all depended on you and pray as if all depended on God."

While our family genetics hail from Africa, Europe, China, and Japan, because of the name I inherited from my father and my oriental features, the Chinese part of us seems to loom large and well out of proportion to their contribution given that none of us has ever had a meaningful relationship with any Chinese relatives, friends, or even acquaintances in my seventy odd years.

Woodlands people gave me their best, and now, hopefully, I have given them my best. So to all who have the occasion to peruse these pages, I hope you enjoy the stories and images I have painted for you. If you are motivated to explore this further, I highly recommend that you travel to Woodlands and sit down with Catalda "Nerissa" Salmon. She is ninety years old and a wonderful storyteller and griot. For US $100, she will sit with you as long as you like and delight you with the stories of old. She may even share her special pot water (soup) with you.

I hope I have also brought honor to my wonderful granny, Mrs. Rosella McKenzie, who saw to my broughtupsy. May she enjoy peaceful rest through eternity. She earned it!

Notes on Jamaican Speak

1.   Any part of the body below the pelvic region is your foot and any part of your limbs below the shoulders is your hand.

2.   We love to repeat words for emphasis. We love a little something extra, added or brata as exemplified in our tautological descriptions. While Americans may say, "Where are you at?" "Déjà vu all over again," "Free gift," "Overexaggerate," "Forward planning," or even "Planning ahead" and "First introduced;" typically Jamaicans will say, "Reverse back," "Rock stone," "Cry eye water," "Mad crazy," "Rain shower," "Lamb meat," and my favorite, "I am all by myself alone."

3.   We do not have "very" in our language. So we just repeat the word as many times to emphasize how serious the circumstances are. I can be sick or I can be sick, sick, sick, or I can be close to dying, when I am sick, sick, sick, sick, sick, sick. The daughter can be pretty, pretty, pretty, pretty, or she can be just pretty. The story is told of a gentleman from Woodlands who migrated to England and became a truck driver. He was backing out into a highway when he was accosted by the police who harshly asked what he was doing. He replied, "Its back back, mi a back back."

4.   If someone in Jamaica asks you for a "drive," we are not asking to drive your car but to get a ride.

5.   While Americans emphasize results, Jamaicans reward effort. Instead of "get dressed"; we say "put on your clothes." In the United States, we wash coffee beans before we put them out to dry. In Jamaica, we "swim" them. Farmers are planters. A rest stop is a "lay by" and a speed bump is a "sleeping policeman." A bright student is "bulby" as in a

bright light bulb. If you want the driver to go faster, you would say "speed up" and Jamaicans say "mash (the gas pedal) e flat" putting the emphasis on the action rather than the desired outcome. You do not hang out clothes to dry; you put them out to sun. "Just be quiet" says Americans or "Resist the temptation to say something you will regret later." We say, "Don't let them pull yu tongue."

6.   It is no big deal for the son from a wealthy family to succeed but we celebrate Horatio Alger stories of a phoenix rising from the ashes. We value remarkable effort regardless of the outcome. You can succeed by failing in Jamaica if you try hard. I witnessed a boy who was trying out for the Jamaican Olympic team to run the mile. The race was over for every one else except he had a lap to go. He got a standing ovation by the spectators.

Basil Waine Kong, Ph.D.,JD

Author's Preface
"Woodlands, Jamaica, gave me my God!"

This story chronicles the life of Garnett Myrie as told to the author. His life mirrors the history of Jamaica from 1953 to 2009 with as much embroidery as my imagination is capable of producing. Yet the remorseless truth is there between the lines and within the reader's own life's experience. If you have any connection to Jamaica, whether "U a bawn ya" (1) or adopted it as a spouse, tourist, or even several generations removed, you will enjoy the story of this rude boy from the hills of Jamaica. In one way or other, Myrie's story is every Jamaican boy's story. A part of Garnett lives in all of us. By reading about his adventures, you will be effectively transformed into "one a wi." (2)

Garnett and I were neighbors. Ms. Rosie in the story is my granny who raised fourteen children of her own and then the two half-china pickney dem (my brother Earl and I). So, before telling this incredible tale, let me first tell you about my own experience growing up in Woodlands, St. Elizabeth from 1947-1959.

When my mother was nineteen years old, she delivered me at Kingston Jubilee Hospital on July 18, 1943. I fell to the floor as none of the nurses or doctors responded to her repeated and exhausted cries for help. While I survived the fall, it was nonetheless a rude awakening. She named me for Basil Rathbone, an English actor who was noted for his pirate characterizations, and my father's last name even though he was married to someone else, and I was off to see the world.

My brother Earl joined us a year later, and we lived together in a house at 15 Jacques Road in the Mountain View section of Kingston until I was four years old. There were frequent visits by my father until his wife's jealousy forced him to abandoned us to return to China. My mother then migrated to the United States, leaving us in the care of her mother (the greatest grandmother the world has ever known). We didn't see our mother again over the next ten years. During this time, however, we wrote to her often. Her letters assured us of her love and inquired about our health and well-being. We, in turn, would just beg her to send us something or other. In her absence, I adopted and regarded all my aunts as my mothers and all my uncles as fathers. In essence, although I had lots of fathers, mothers, uncles and aunts at age twelve, I could not have identified either my genetic father or mother in a police line-up.

I believe, however, that we were never out of our mother's thoughts. She sent a money order each and every month and a parcel with clothes and toys about six times per year. The members of the community would see us carrying these packages from the Springfield Post Office and jealously comment that more "breguede" had arrived. One of the exciting items in one of the parcels was a gramophone. It was a marvel that attracted a great deal of attention as people wondered how the musicians got into the box to make the sound. As time went on, my brother's curiosity got the better of him, and he broke it looking for the musicians inside. That was the end of our musical interludes.

I remember my granny marking the size and shape of our feet on paper, cutting and sending the imprint to my mother so that she could send back shoes. When the shoes came, if they were too big, I would stuff them with paper until I grew into them. If they were too small, we would fill them with dry corn and dipped them in water. As the corn expanded, so did the shoes. The corn was then made into hominy for breakfast.

I left the people I loved most and the village that raised me to go to 'merica on April 3, 1959. The day we arrived in New York via Avianca Airways, it was cold and snowing. Meeting my new father and brothers for the first time signaled that there were going to be a lot of adjustments in our thinking and experience. Our younger brothers (Robbie and Kevin Johnson) had to get used to sharing their Mom, their rooms and their toys. At least for the first three months, Mom was extremely attentive and showered us with her time, her cooking, her guidance, and her tutoring. In addition to all the ice cream, Jell-O, and cakes we could eat, she tended to the concerted cultivation of our skills and talents.

I ate in a restaurant for the first time at fifteen years old when she took us to see, hear, and feel the pulse of New York City including seeing it from the Empire State Building. This was both exciting and intimidating. Our necks ached as we could not stop looking up at the tall buildings. I was impressed by the lights on Broadway, the man smoking camel cigarettes, the George Washington Bridge, the Lincoln Tunnel, and the number of automobiles, the sight of which reminded me of an ant's nest. I had come a long way from Woodlands.

When we started attending Morristown High School, we only spoke deep country patois that no one understood, and we obviously could not decipher what Americans said either. We became exhausted having to repeat ourselves to no avail as people continually asked, "What did you say?" And we responded, "A wa yu a sa?" It took a minute to recognize that talking slower and louder was not helpful. One of my teachers asked me if I believed everything I read, and true to my upbringing, I said yes. Why would they write something that wasn't true? She enlightened me.

I then reflected on my experience at the Denbeigh Show when I watched a weight lifter with the body of Adonis reach a weight that he could not handle, but after he went to a Guinness booth and heartily drank a stout, he returned to easily hoist the stubborn weight over his head to great applause. I have been trying to get that magic strength ever since by consuming lots of Guinness. I remember that an argument could be easily won by just showing your opponent that it was written in the Gleaner or the Bible. In fact, I believed the Gleaner was the bible.

My mother quickly recognized our severe educational deficits and hired a language teacher, a piano teacher, a math teacher, and a writing teacher—we were kept busy. She even sent us to a psychiatrist to help us with our adjustment when out of sheer frustration, "wata come a wi eye," (3) and we both demanded to be sent back to the idyllic life we remembered in Jamaica. What we missed most was a community of people who cared. Other than our immediate family, we felt like no one else in America cared.

In the mornings, we got dressed, went to school, participated in sports after school and then to tutors before coming home, eating, doing the dishes and our homework, and going to sleep exhausted. Mom's strategy was to keep us busy and out of trouble.

We went to the Morristown YMCA often and learned to swim, do gymnastics, play basketball, and just play with other children. I once fell on my head doing the rings in gymnastics—no problem. I have been developing a hard head from the moment I was born and from the school of hard knocks. While I was otherwise a talented athlete, I never got the knack for basketball or football. However, there was never a time when I was not involved in varsity sports. I lettered and excelled in track (set a 400 meter school record in 50.3 seconds), soccer, cross-country, and especially wrestling. The Kong brothers were both district champion wrestlers. I wrestled at the 122 weight class. I have gained one pound each year since then.

When my sixteenth birthday approached, my mother realized that I had never celebrated a birthday, so she decided that she would give me a special party. The problem was that I had just arrived in the United States and did not know anyone other than family and the few neighbors on our block. So I invited everybody I encountered at school. On the night of the party, hundreds of kids showed up, and my mother had to bar the door and only allowed twenty people to come into the house while very upset kids who were asking for the free food I promised lingered in the street in front of our house. On that memorable birthday, I received my first-ever birthday presents: a briefcase, a Webcore tape recorder, and a Phillips transistor radio.

Mom was active in the civil rights movement. In addition to supporting the movement, she worked with a group to integrate rental properties. She even invited me to speak up in these gatherings in our living room. The black women would try to rent homes and were told that it was rented but when the white women applied, they were accepted and offered the same apartment. Their activities lead to equal housing legislation in New Jersey.

My mother personally taught us to drive her 1957 Chevrolet and took us to caddy at Springbrook Country Club on weekends. We had to save everything we earned. I learned to play golf at sixteen when a member gave me an old set of clubs, and we were allowed to play on caddy day each Monday. I now play regularly to a fourteen handicap. I am frustrated that after playing golf for fifty years, this is as good as I get. I am told in Jamaica that "golf doesn't live in anybody's yard."

My stepfather, Arthur Johnson, worked for Ford Motor Company, had a generous heart, and always drove the latest model Cadillac. He took us fishing and to the race track, taught us to pitch horse shoes, and to play baseball. He played poker with us, and we often enjoyed a beer together. To my mother's disgust, he would never ask for directions, and we were always lost in our travels but he was good at fixing cars and appliances. He regaled us daily with his World War II stories and told us that the United States is a land of opportunity and how we could achieve great things if we put our minds and hearts into whatever we wanted to do. He wanted me to play professional baseball as he once played in the Negro baseball league.

Marcus Garvey's "Back to Africa" movement was in full swing when my mother was born on December 16, 1922, to William and Rosella McKenzie. In 1938, after leaving Springfield School, she was sent to Kingston to live with her Sister Myrtle and find work so she could help support her siblings after her father (William McKenzie) died suddenly of a heart attack. She soon buck upon (4) Chan Kong (her employer) with whom she had two children. When Chan unexpectedly returned to China, she had to "turn hand and make fashion." (5) She took her two boys to live with her mother and went off to the United States on a two week visa. When a gentleman in Kingston found out that she was going to New York, he gave her a bottle of Appleton over-proof rum to give to his war buddy who lived in New Jersey. Soon after arriving in the United States, she diligently made her way to New Jersey and delivered the rum.

Upon their meeting, Mr. Arthur Johnson immediately became intoxicated by her beauty. They fell in love, and in a world wind of activity, were married ten days later on May 26, 1948. The union produced two more boys (Robbie and Kevin). Arthur and Violet lived happily together for fifty years. Unfortunately, because Arthur was a heavy smoker (a habit he picked up from receiving free cigarettes as a soldier in Uncle Sam's Army during World War II), he died from lung cancer in 1997. When he was asked if he knew how to play Bid Whist, (6) he is fondly remembered as saying, "Who do you think put the bid in Whist?"

When I was graduating from Dickinson Law School, My mother's comment was "Son, you know how proud I am for all you have done with your life, but aren't you concerned that lawyers can't go to Heaven?" She was serious.

My mother had a wonderful sense of humor. I am a great advocate for organ transplantation and talked my mother into signing her driver's license authorizing doctors to harvest her organs if and when she died. While she eventually agreed, her initial response was that it is clearly un-Christian to be buried without all her organs. "What if," she said, "Lazarus had donated his organs when he died and the Lord came and commanded: 'Lazarus, raise come!' Lazarus would have fi say: 'mi can't come you know sah. Wa mi fi do? (7) They take everything.' And the Lord would have fi say: 'Dog nam yu supper Lazarus. Sorry fi you'". (8)

She was an avid reader of "Reader's Digest" and on every visit, she would regale us with a story which I would then repeat in my talks across the country when I served as the CEO of the Association of Black Cardiologists. This was my favorite: A husband and wife decided to take a trip to the Holy Land (Israel). When her mother learned about their plans, she pleaded with them to allow her to accompany them. At first, he objected. But she prevailed by convincing them how meaningful it would be for her as she faithfully studied the New Testament and she would love to see all the places where Jesus walked. While on the trip, the three of them were having a glorious time when unfortunately, the mother had a heart attack and died. While bewildered and not knowing what to do, the hotel manager suggested that they call the American embassy. The ambassador was very sympathetic and suggested the following options. "In Israel, burials are very efficient and would cost less than $2,000. If you ship the body back to the United States, it is likely to cost $20,000 when you add up all the costs. What would you like to do?" The husband responded: "Ambassador, I am taking my mother-in-law back to the United States for a proper burial no matter how much it cost." When the Ambassador asked why, he responded: "Look, two thousand years ago, didn't they burry someone here and he came back? I have never heard of anyone buried in the United States coming back. I just want to make sure."

I grew up singing "God Bless Our Gracious Queen" (9) with great reverence at all public events until I left Jamaica at the tender age of fifteen, lived in the United States for fifty years where I was a lawyer, psychologist, university professor, hospital administrator and most noticeably, as the chief executive officer of the Association of Black Cardiologists in Atlanta for twenty one years. I returned in 2008 singing "Eternal Father, Bless Our Land." (10) While I was away, I visited Jamaica about twenty times, the first ten times to visit family but after the death of my granny and the Manley era migration (11) in the 1980s to England, Canada, and the United States, my wife and I didn't have family to visit, so we stayed in hotels. As an avid golfer, Jamaica is always a feast—so many great golf courses, so little time!

After Granny died, I bought the ten-acre family farm from my aunts and uncles. It now limps along without the vigor of the old days when we regularly harvested yams, coco, dashine, coffee, pimento (cloves), cassava, breadfruit, ackee, bananas, carrots, cabbage, corn, peas as well as raised cows, pigs, goats, and chickens. Unlike American farms that usually specialize in one product, ours try to be self-sufficient and grow a little of everything. Now, instead of cane, however, I grow dukane, a nuisance plant that sucks up the water in my pond. The property is nevertheless beautiful to the eye and restful to the spirit.

Woodlands District is difficult to find on a map or driving. No one ever accidently comes across it. It will be found, however, in the souls of everyone who were fortunate enough to have lived there. We love to keep company. Believing that the aim of life is to find good company, as I travel around the world, this is one of the characteristics I inherited from Woodlands: I initiate conversations with whoever is at hand.

Ninety nine percent of Americans have never killed an animal for food. Some years ago, I was amused that when a surveyor asked a sample of Americans where meat and milk came from. They answered: "The Supermarket"! Kingston Ginals (12) fall into that category as well. I am going to guess that all country boys, however, grew up knowing how to test if a chicken is about to lay an egg, milking cows and goats, hunting birds, watching chickens run around with their heads cut off, cows falling after being poled on the back of their necks, goats hanging by their hind legs with their life blood draining from them and pigs being stabbed in the heart. I was asked some years ago if everything went to hell, could my family and I survive in the wild. I have no doubt that I could, and it would not just be from eating berries. Growing up in the country taught us survival skills. My cousin, Presley, says he always grow some callaloo (13) as he believed that if he had to, he could live on it for a long time, cooked or raw.

If I had fallen asleep fifty years ago and recently woke up, I would find that Woodlands District has mostly gone backward. Under the rural development initiative of Prime Minister Michael Manley, most people in our district now have access to electricity but they pay dearly for it. Many people have computers and cell phones are a necessity for immediate access to friends and relatives near and far. Jamaicans love to talk. Thanks to the policies of the wireless companies, there is no cost to those receiving calls, only the caller is charged. So the Grannies of Woodlands can keep in touch with their children and grand pickney dem who are living in town (14) or foreign.

After successful careers, some people return to build "Been to" houses (15) and own automobiles. The beautiful new road from Mocho to Springfield thru Woodlands is a gift from whatever Gods may be. I smile broadly whenever I make the right turn from Mocho. We suffered through an eternity of extremely bad roads, and now it is smooth sailing on Barber Greene. (16) May Allah be praised.

The returning "been to" people (who spent time in England, 'merica, and Canada) are now highly invested in community development but they pay a tremendous price because they invariably return without their children and grandchildren. Here is my version of the frustrations and dilemma of the Jamaican Diaspora that I call, "Cotching in Atlanta":

I didn't come to 'merica to stay
I only came to learn and earn a little money
To go back home to build a house, buy a car and maybe a bar
But I now have seven grand pickney here
Who don't know the joys and have no interest in the place I call yard (17)
I yearn for the Rock but the rock won't have me
While I am cotching (18) in Atlanta, my heart is in Jamaica
I don't want to stay but I cannot go home
See me daya (19) between the sheets of the bed I made
With no idea where the grass is greener
I try to duplicate Jamaica in Atlanta but the patties are neither Tastee or Juici (20)
I play dominoes, drink rum punch and Red Stripe Beer
I can eat escovitch fish, curry goat and rice, but it's not Cooshues (21)

I can get fried fish, bammy and festival, but it's not at Hellshire Beach (22)
I scream for run raisin ice cream, but it's not from Devon House (23)
I watch cricket matches but it's not at Sabina Park (24)
I read the Atlanta Journal Constitution but it is not the Gleaner (25)
I enjoy all the comforts of home but it no home
I miss Mass Bertie, Mother Blake, Uncle Benji, Brother Boogs and Aunt Poochos
Greeting me with "mawnin" and "God bless you" when I share what I have with them
Sorrel (26) and fruitcake in December only make me long for Father Christmas (27)
I don't want a "Merry Christmas" I want a "Happy Christmas"
I can watch 200 channels on my TV but find nothing to watch
Instead of pumpkin beef soup on Saturdays, I now eat hotdogs and beans.
Mi Belly full but mi hungry.

Even though my wife and I live in Kingston, we have to frequently fly to various destination to attend the birth of a child, a graduation, a wedding, a birthday, anniversary, Thanksgiving, a recital or school related performances, as well as other important family occasions that we try not to miss. It isn't easy balancing these obligations with life in Jamaica. My wife and I also love to travel to distant shores, and we continue to visit four countries per year but eventually we want to just come home, drop anchor, and rest our bones in Jamaica. After visiting one hundred countries, with all our woes, "no where no better than yard." And if Woodlands District only had a golf course, "nowhere in Jamaica would be better than Woodlands."

In 1958, I was the Boy's Sports Champion at Springfield All Age School and Ms. Erma Cameron was the Girls' Champion. A year later, I left for 'merica, and she went to England where she became a sales assistant. We have both returned but to her credit, she built a fine house in Woodlands and I am living in Kingston.

She is now prominent in Church and Community affairs. I was most sympathetic to her situation as she built her house next to a gentleman who believed he was a radio DJ and blasted her with his loud music night and day. He stubbornly refused to cease being a nuisance even after the District Constable was called a dozen times about it. They finally confiscated his equipment. My Aunt, Myra McDonald, migrated to the United States soon after I returned to Jamaica and is now residing with her children in Pennsylvania and Texas. I hope these two events were not connected.

On one of my frequent visits to the Kingston home of my childhood friend, Garnett Myrie suggested that I write his life story with elaborate descriptions of our boyhood experiences. "I will reveal my most precious memories like a mother passing on jewels to her children. The story of my life should be told. Let's not leave this unworded."

His family property and mine abut each other so we came under the same influences and enjoyed the same experiences although Garnett is ten years younger. Who else could do justice to his life story? I immediately saw the possibilities, got on my computer and started to write down everything he dictated to me. The many hours we spent reminiscing about his life was pure joy. What a fascinating life it turned out to be!

On each visit back to Woodlands, people are genuinely happy to greet me back home, eagerly reminding me of the role they played in my broughtupsy. (28) My laughter had vigor as they reminded me about what I was like as a little man. I indulge myself in whatever they offered: a glass of cool water, a drink of rum, and a piece of cake, curry goat, lemonade made with sour oranges, fruits picked from trees in their yard—and especially carrot juice. I cannot get enough. As I go from house to house to visit, it is one sensation after another as my teeth are never idle. So much food is offered, I leave suspecting that I have left a famine in my wake. They remember with gratitude the many kindnesses of my granny and the fond memories of the two half china pickney dem. The hospitality is always appreciated. As I walk about, I again smell the fennel, mint, kuss kuss, orange blossoms, and fever (lemon) grass that never fails to intoxicate my senses. As a customary courtesy to returning sons and daughters, I was invited to account for myself at Springfield Moravian Church during services where I was overwhelmed with hugs and kisses.

I reminded everyone that I was the same "Ms. Rosie grand pickney" and pointed out where we sat each Sunday and that the lessons I learned in our community had served me well as I negotiated my way though life. I had returned to Jamaica and working as the president of the Heart Institute of the Caribbean Foundation in Kingston. I introduced my guest from the "Food for the Poor" who had agreed with urging from Mr. Garnett Myrie and I to build 150 houses for the people in our community. As a token of their commitment to Woodlands, they delivered wheelchairs to help those who could not walk. I was also able to announce that within two months, we had arranged for a large health fair when well baby and physical and dental exams would be done by my wife as well as a group of physicians from the United States. They would find free eye glasses and medication useful.

On reflection, after fifty years, I had to use a lot of imagination to remember the grove of trees from the stumps remaining. I was looking at mere fragments of the good old days but delighted in conjuring up the luster of times past. I was still able to paint a landscape on a canvas that glowed with pretty pictures of my school days as well as the willows singing and dancing in the breeze, sports day, abundant and colorful birds chirping and darting about and the glow of the flower gardens in front of each house.

Life in Woodlands was idyllic in the old days. It was truly egalitarian as there were no rich or poor people. While most of our food, toys, clothes and tools were homegrown and handmade, I recall (with pardonable vanity), the visits of my school mates who shared my store bought toys, gramophone and bicycle, compliments of my mother. My brother and I had several pairs of shoes as well as pus (sneakers). It thrills me to remember the sense of freedom I enjoyed as we roamed the bush in search of friends, fruits in season, fire wood for our kitchens and hunting birds with catapults—all without adult supervision.

On one of my visits, I encountered a school mate from Springfield All Age School. Other than Miss Erma Cameron, my other friends from my youth were all seeking their fortunes elsewhere. Unfortunately, this classmate (Egbert) was the one boy with whom I had several school yard fights over what I cannot remember. I do remember squaring off in a boxing position uncertain as to whether to proceed to blows but not knowing how to get out of it. Some trouble maker would pick up some small stones and challenged one of us into knocking the stones out of his hands and get on with the fight. "Hot pepper, hot pepper, box and touch." Our fighting stopped when my younger brother who was more strapin (29) than I, entered the fray and humiliated him on my behalf. But here we were, fifty years later, full of cheerfulness. We recognized each other simultaneously, hugged and no animosity existed between us. "Rahted, it no Basil Kong dat?" "Kiss mi neck, Egbert?"

As he was gazing with a lecherous eye at the rum bar across the street, I invited him to have a drink with me. We were joined by others as we continued to talk and wet our whistles.

I drank Red Stripe beers, and he ordered John Crow Batty. The bartender explained that it is the raw over proof rum that employees at the Appleton Estate pour into their water boots or soak in crocus bags, (30) walk out of the factory passing the gate inspections and later pour the liquid into basins and then into old bottles, stinking feet notwithstanding, to be shared with friends or sold to their local rum shops.

Egbert and I recalled our school days and what so and so were doing and where they lived. Mostly the answer was "Dem gone foreign and never come back." He had stuck with farming and went to 'merica to do farmwork. While he never married, he had fathered four children. When I explained that I had returned to Jamaica to live. He thought this was preposterous and asked most sincerely, "Are you mad? Everyone in Jamaica is trying to get the hell away from this godforsaken country, and you come back. You are mad. You no see Jamaica mash up?"

The same way john crow batty wiped away the stench from stinking toes, time healed our disagreements, and we only spoke about the good times, our athletic contests, and even when he beat me at ping-pong with the sand paddles on the table we built and painted under the direction of Mr. Ronald Essen, the woodshop teacher. He regretted that children no longer had manual training so they can do carpentry. After an hour, we parted with a sincere good bye and a promise to keep in touch.

The people I visited used to laugh so spontaneously and found humor in everything. They are now sullen and beaten down with the hard life. Unruly children dressed in rags reminded me of sackcloth and ashes. The young men were weighted down by hopelessness and blighted dreams while older men were just tired out from back breaking unrequited toil. They seem burdened down with the present and indifferent to the future with no hopes or interests. Crippled old people with no visible means of support who survive only by the kindness of neighbors. For a lot of reasons, our district has been reduced to "a village of tears."

Woodlands even had our first violent crime. The adorable, generous, and community minded Ms. Kareen Lawson who made a success of herself in 'merica and was coming home for Christmas (2008) with great joy in her heart. Unfortunately, she was followed by criminals as she departed Montego Bay Airport in a rented car loaded with presents for family, friends and the children of the community. When she stopped at Woodlands Crossroads to greet family, the criminals alighted from their car with guns and demanded that she surrender her car with all the presents. When she adamantly refused, they shot her and took the car. She returned to the United States paralyzed with a broken heart. But she could not stay away from the love of her family, so she returned and the community made up for it with all the love they could muster. It is a sad story, but at least the perpetrators where not from Woodlands.

Although St. Elizabeth is the breadbasket of Jamaica because of our rich soil and abundant rain, we are without commerce or manufacturing. Other than remittances from loved ones abroad, day labor, selling fruits and vegetables and raising a few chickens, pigs, goats and cows, there are no other tangible means of support. A man confessed to me that couldn't read or write because his parents never sent him to school and told him that he only needed to know how to dig a yam hill to get by, except now he cannot find any land to plant his ground. I cursed our government for neglecting these basic needs of our citizens. And yet, they survive—some even thrive. I promise to keep on protesting and make personal sacrifices to better their condition.

In days of old, when darkness descended, we lit the kerosene lamp, wiped the soot from the previous night with a piece of old Gleaner, and replaced the glass shade back in the prongs around the flame. My brother and I then went out to Mass Claudie's shop for our favorite beverage, to hear the latest jokes, listen to the Telefunkin radio that was tuned to a station in New Orleans. This was our introduction to Rock and Roll. We played dominoes or a card game we called All Fours ("High, Low, Jack, Game"). We didn't have dice so we used broken porcelain dinner plates and made one inch rounded chips that were blank on one side and the flowers on the other. We took turns throwing them on the ground like dice. The winner at each turn was the player who showed the most flowers. On our way home from the shop, we carried a nip of brandy that Granny drank just before she went to bed.

The beds my brother and I slept in were so lumpy we had hill and gully rides throughout the night. We moved the dried banana leaves around and simmered down until we felt the filling hugging us. Sometimes we could find the exact spot we left from morning. It was so cozy we did not need a blanket. We awoke snuggled in our nest as soon as the cock crowed, got up totally refreshed and feeling frisky. We joined Granny on our knees beside the bed for our morning prayers, walked the fifty yards to use the two seat outdoor toilet before bathing together like naked birds in the water that had collected in the wooden tub that we pretended was a boat.

While we took our bath beside the house, both men and women would walk through our yard, and we felt no embarrassment or modesty being naked before them. Not far away, Granny would throw corn to the chickens and their heads would bob up and down as they filled their craw and cooed to each other. Throughout the day, Granny would check if a hen would lay an egg that day. They would spend the day scratching for worms and otherwise swallowing pebbles and anything else that was shiny. When they were killed for Sunday dinner, my brother and I would anxiously cut into their gizzards to see what strange objects they had swallowed.

For breakfast, my favorite was a hunk (31) of corn pone and hot milk. Granny made the best corn pone with bits of chewy coconut. She baked it in a Dutch pot (32) with piles of hot coals on top and bottom. Each time she baked, she would remark, "Hell a top. Hell a bottom. Hallelujah in the middle." We always got a thrill out of her repeating that. While the hot scald milk was a constant as children were not allowed to have coffee, it was either accompanied by hard dough bread, Johnny cakes, bullahs, hard or soft boiled eggs (that she served in little egg cups), ackee, and salt fish. Since we also like to have dinner for breakfast, anything left over from dinner is served for breakfast. On Saturday mornings, we got corn meal porridge (pap) with condensed sweet milk. For lunch, we had the rest of the porridge that had congealed. We turned it upside down to appreciate the shiny bottom.

If we could subtract the drug dealing, murders, and abuse of modern Dons, I happen to believe a Village Chief, "Big Man" or Don is not only needed but desirable. My model was Mass Claudie McDonald (my uncle) who was the big man of Woodlands. He was a tremendous resource. He owned the "Shop" in Woodlands that served as the center of the life of the community. When politicians (regardless of party) gave speeches, he provided the Tilley lamp (33) and the space. Every Sunday evening, an evangelical church met under the eves of the shop with their spirited songs, drums, and sermons. The cricket club met in the storage room sitting on crocus bags that were full with dried pimento and coffee and sewed shut with a long curved needle and coarse thread to be sold to the merchant trucks that came by each week.

Men bought drinks in the bar, shared the latest news, gossiped and socialized. He had the only public toilet in the district. When some of the young men from Woodlands migrated to England and sent back to tell the others that there were jobs waiting for them, it was Claudie McDonald who bought their land or whatever they wanted to sell to make up their fare. He also loaned money to several who promised to repay him as soon as they got paid in England. No one reneged on these promises. The most important service he provided, however, was advice. Even though he only had an elementary school education, he was respected as a man who "knows things," and what he didn't know, he could decipher. He acted as a mediator for the purchase and sale of livestock and property and knew the exact contact if anyone from Woodlands wanted to do business with someone in Kingston, Montego Bay or anywhere throughout the Island. It helped that his wife, Miss. Myra, ran the "Woodlands PA" Postal Agency.

Without telephones, cell phones e-mail or even messengers, this informal network of "Big men" from each community served not only their economic interests but those who they chose to favor with this access. No employer would give a job to anyone without the recommendation of one of these Dons. Dr. Hibbert owned two drug stores—one in New Market and the other in Springfield where he lived. He and his wife, Jemima, could cook up a concoction for every disease from the one thousand jars of herbs in his shop. They also made wonderful wedding cakes. Their daughter (Grace Darling Hibbert) migrated to England and had the distinction of serving as a pilot in the Royal Air Force. Other big men I knew included Amos Kirlew from Backstreet, Lenny Miles in Santa Cruz, John McKenzie in Mile Gully in Manchester, Lynn Salmon and Noel Black in Springfield, Mr. Cummings in New Market, Sidney Hamilton and Charlie Baby in Bottom Roads.

Mass Claudie not only gave paradise plums (34) to all the pickney who stopped in the shop, gave store credit for groceries as well as a cool drink of water for travelers. In fact, for six pence, a traveler could buy two ounces of sugar; pick a sour orange out back, make delicious lemonade as well as buy a bun with an ounce of cheese or bread with butter. For about a shilling, a traveler could buy a can of sardine or salmon and even a tin of bully beef spiced up with free scotch bonnet or bird pepper from trees under the window of the shop. You could also buy a bulla (35) or hard dough bread by the slice.

In the 1950s, before the great migration to England, we could lively up ourselves with Saturday night dances with Herbie

Arnold's Rumba Band (with Neri Myrie, John Bishop playing guitars, James Smith strumming the banjo while Wepi and Little Man took turns with the Rumba Box), Mr. Bernard played he drums, Manbalm played the fife. We enjoyed Pinnock's domino tournaments and even cockfights sponsored by "Jancrow Can" as well as regular cricket matches with Captain Mills at the helm.

Captain Mills loved cricket, and when he learned that a one-ton iron roller that was filled with concrete to smooth the cricket pitch was available twenty miles away in Lacovia, he organized a team of men and donkies to bring it back to Woodlands. They tied the ropes to the handle of the roller to the harness of the three donkies forming a troika and towed the roller to Woodlands, a trip that took two days. It was a cause for celebration and a source of great pride to the community when they arrived back in Woodlands like men returning from war. Plenty road was smoothed out as the heavy roller made its way to Woodlands.

Even with the blessings and magic of Bunda, the Obeahman, who scattered chicken blood by the stumps, I clearly remember the cricket match against New Market when this batter (a policeman) was abusing us against the best spin bowling of Bra Bone (Joslyn Mills) and Herbie Arnold, the fast bowler. Neville Cameron's balls were described as "living fire." Just as we began to feel let down by this amazing batsman from New market, Bunny (Erthan Billings) caught a well hit ball close to the boundary up on the hillside close to the bamboo grove, I believe you could have heard the shouting and celebration up at church yard a mile away. Sidney Curlew hit a six over the wall that fell in Mass Austin's ground among the dashine and Coco. Ronnie McKenzie caught a ball on the slip. Courtney Phillips didn't break the egg (36) but Austin Heron, Little Man, Bertie Barrett, Alto Ferguson, Samuel Cameron, Basil Cameron and Arthur Blake scored about ten runs each to beat New Market. When we won (as the Obeah man predicted) they were all heroes, and the women denied them nothing. The home team treated the visitors to all the beer they could drink as well as curry goat and white rice. These treats were all paid for by the profit Mass Claudie made from the paying customers. White over proof rum, three dagger rum and Red Stripe beer flowed freely. So was hot green tea! There was no drinking age so I was not only working in the shop selling liquor but drank with the men when I was only twelve.

The after cricket dance was held in a temporary dance hall built for the occasion with a dirt floor, coconut bows and bamboo sides under the stars. Herbie Arnold and the rest of the band changed from their white cricket uniforms to colorful shirts to lick the music till midnight. I remember taking turns playing the rumba box but I didn't last as it hurt my fingers. But I also took turns dancing with older women.

My most delightful image is getting on the truck to go home after a victorious match when we would rub in the defeat on the vanquished. As we departed, we sang with great vigor, "You were wrong to send and call us, you were wrong . . ." And as the feelings and laughter got higher and higher. We sang a popular song at the time:

"Cricket, lovely cricket,
at Lord's where I saw it.
Cricket, lovely cricket,
at Lord's where I saw it.
Yardley tried his best
but Goddard won the Test.
They gave the crowd plenty fun.
Second Test and West Indies won
with those little pals of mine,
Ramadhin and Valentine."(Lord Beginner, 1950)

I am actually amazed that a small village in the most rural part of Jamaica could have been so organized and advanced. The secret was our cricket team. Many larger towns like Springfield, Donegal, Brighton, and Mocho did not have an organized cricket club with all the equipment and expertise like Woodlands. Outstanding athletes like Little Man, Spirit, Ronnie Ferguson, Bertie Barrett, Amos Smith, Mass Hugh Cameron, Georgie and Uncle Paul Ferguson, Aston Heron and Edwin Gooden, who was so engaging, everyone just called him "Polite." Even Uncle Claudie tried but had limited ability. The glue that held it all together was a highly respected old gentleman who was loved by everyone. Captain Mills arranged for all the games as far away as Success, Round Hill, Brooks Park, Balaclava, Ipswich, Santa Cruz, Wales Pond and New Market, conducted practice, kept records and was an inspiration for the entire community in his quiet assertive manner. Cricket meetings strictly followed Roberts Rules of Order, and he never had to raise his voice.

It is worth telling that when we went on a cricket outing to Lucie, we came back with one more passenger. Pinnock met a woman (Sybil) at the social after the match, and he talked her into moving back to Woodlands with him. She fell in love, went home, packed her clothes in a wicker basket, got on the truck and ended up in a happy, successful marriage producing a daughter they named Miss P. Wedding bliss lasted until Miss Sybil died forty years later, and he followed her to a grave beside her two years after. In addition to running a shop, they organized domino tournaments; Saturday night dances; farmed, owned a Leland Truck that hauled the cricket team as well as the farmers and their loads to market in New Market, Montego Bay, Black River, and even Kingston.

As a member of the Boys Brigade Cricket Team, I can still feel the joy of the one six I hit in a game against the Boys Brigade in Magotty. The ball went to my left, and instinctively, I turned and caught the ball just right, and it sailed over the boundary. The thrill of that knock has remained and I am reminded of it every time I attend a cricket match and even with the mention of the word "cricket." Unfortunately, I was bowled out by the very next ball. In golf, we call it a PBSU (Post Birdie Screw Up).

In those days, only Minister Hayden Todd had a car. Half the boys packed into the car while the other half started walking for our twenty mile journey to play cricket. The first group was let off at the fifteen mile point and Minister Todd would return to pick up the group who were walking at the ten mile point and take them to the destination, and on the way back, the groups would reverse the process. As the car passed the group who had been driven the first leg of the trip, I hopped onto the back of the car and held on for dare life. I didn't realize that he could see me in his side mirror. When Rev. Todd realized I was there, he stopped the car and with his face turning a bright red with anger, cursed me with his British ascent. I don't understand exactly what he said, but he was not thinking kind thoughts and may have temporarily surrendered his ministerial collar.

Children had free access to all the fruit trees in our community. Mother Blake had the juiciest, sweetest and largest tangerines. Ms Edna Wright was famous for jackfruit as well as her three beautiful daughters. Mango was abundant so we spent many hours seeking out the crusty ones that were the sweetest. Mass Benji had a forest of guava that ended up as guava jelly. He had a hundred acres, so star apples, sweet cup, June plums, rose plums, neaseberrys as well as a pond where we went to splash in the cool water. We were forbidden to go back to the pond after one of our friends drowned when he got entangled in the bamboo that had fallen into the pond. Many a belly bottom bun. Since we knew nothing of the germ theory or micro organisms, the cows and all of us drank the cool shade tree water we swam in. As much as I have traveled through Africa, Mexico, South America and Asia, I have never had intestinal issues because of the bacteria already living in my stomach. If it doesn't kill you, it makes you stronger.

In 1957, the Minister of Education wanted to introduce the children of Jamaica to movies. So he sent a team in a van to show movies at schools throughout the land. My first movie was: "Seven Brides for Seven Brothers". They then showed the "Life of Jesus Christ." As we did not know there were such things as "actors", we actually believed we were eye witnesses to the stories. We cried for days and were inspired to live the life Jesus had commanded us to live.

My comrades from school included Hiram Woodstock, Lynval Coke, Sylvester Meir, Elaine Lyons, Faye James, Branford Roy Robinson and Ruby Stewart, who later married. My limited information on their whereabouts tell me that they are all well off but not necessarily happy, because, for economic reasons, they are living in the various corners of the globe. I was traveling through Miami ten years ago and listening to a radio show about insurance. The very elegant host was "Mr. Roy Robinson." As he gave the number to call for more information, I called, and it turned out to be the same Blanford. We met for lunch and had a delightful time. He was a big success with his own insurance firm. Unfortunately, he and Ruby had divorced.

When I attended Madison High School in the United States, I ran the risk of never going to college because I was judged to have excellent skills working my hand in wood. Half the shed across the road on Springfield Moravian Church property, was used to house the horses that the men rode to church or when Mrs. Billings rode her white horse to school. The other half served as our wood shop. Under the supervision of Mr. Ronald Essen, we learned to saw, plane, sand, fit joints, glue, nail, varnish, made breakfast trays, picture frames, shields to award to winners of various contests, tables, chairs, bed frames and even doors and windows. We even made our own ping-pong table that was a great source of enjoyment for all of us. So while I was very average in my academic subjects after I moved to the United States, I was the most outstanding student in wood shop.

So my guidance counselor advised me to develop this talent and apprentice with a carpenter she knew. I obsessed over this decision, but because I had set a four-hundred yard track record, Simpson College in Indianola, Iowa, offered me a scholarship. So I decided to go to college. Even though I love the smell of cedar and the beauty of Blue Mahoe, I have not used a saw or planed a piece of wood since then.

Digging Matches or Morning work were special days in Woodlands. When someone wanted to plough and box his land for planting carrots, cabbage or Irish potatoes, instead of paying laborers, he invited all the men in the community to morning report and hired a singer man who kept the men in rhythm with digging songs like "Draw Mattie out of bush mouth." "Gal and Boy down a manual road to brock rock stone. Brock them one by one. Brock them two by two." "Day O, Day O, Day da light and me wan go home," and "Chi Chi Bud Oh. Some a dem a halla, some a bawl." "Baba Ram goat Oh, Baba daya." The women cooked corn meal dumplings the size of cartwheels, fried corn pork, dasheen, yam, bananas as well as fry up salt fish with callaloo that was served on Banana leaves. The children served the water, and everyone dipped in the pail and drank from the same tourine. After the work was done, tired and satisfied, they would marvel at what they could accomplish when they worked together.

Among the industries in our community in the fifties was a wet sugar factory around Friendship (Just beyond Shields's Pon.) Mass Aston Curlew and Captain Mills bought Euba cane from others in the district, gathered them in big piles, prasup his mule to the grinder and sent him blindfolded around endless circles while Mass Aston jammed the sugar cane between the two large steel rollers. The greenish cane juice extracted in this way would run down into barrels creating white foam on top. If we were lucky, Mass Aston would allow us to dip up some of the cane juice and drink all we wanted. After a while, we would be staggering around from the sugar high. The cane juice was transferred to the big copper pots with a big fire with the dried cane trash that he called bagasse. He constantly skimmed the fraught and stirred the juice until it became thick. Again, this wet sugar would be a treat as Mass Aston would let us dip up some when it cooled. He even had some ginger to mix with the wet sugar. He would pour the wet sugar in used and washed up "kerosene" or butter pans and took it to New Market to sell on Wednesdays or Saturdays by the quart for one and six. The factory ended with Mass Aston's death, and there is now no sign of this once-thriving enterprise.

So, in addition to the carpentry shop run by the Myrie Brothers, the sugar factories run by Mass Austin Curlew and Captain Mills, the leather tanning operation by the Bromleys, and the building expertise of Chiphus and Clif. Banton who built water tanks and houses that are still standing after our many hurricanes, the butcher shop run by Mr. John Johnson and Mr. Manley, the bakery owned by Mr. Harry Chen See, the cigar factory run by Ms. Euda McKenzie who used the bark of mahoe to make rope and even made rope tobacco that Mass Claudie would sell by the inch so the men could fill their pipes and smoke it. Basil and Jimmy Graves cut trees and sawed up lumber with long saws, and when the saws were no longer useful, they cut them into machetes. Mr. Alberga Robinson could turn a tin can into a coffee mug, a horse shoeing operation run by Rufus Heron and Brother Boogs, Lady Champion buses as well as a truck to transport goods to market run by Victor Marshall and Charlie Smith; ice cream, and snowballs sold by Spirit on Sundays and holidays. We had a thriving community.

There is no longer a cricket pitch, no live music, no horses to race at Shield Pond and the large copper pots that boiled sugar has been sold off as antiques. While progress has been made with electricity, roads, radio, television, and communications, the community has reverted to small farms. Sunday attendance at Springfield Moravian church has been reduced from three hundred to fifty. There are no May Poles, Merry-go-rounds or any form of entertainment, except television, computer games, and talking on cell phones. Unfortunately, those who remain don't even bother to socialize with each other like the old days.

On my way back to Kingston after a visit to Woodlands, I look out at the hectares of land which now lie dormant but, in my youth, had been packed with the lifeblood of our community: fruit trees and flowers, coconuts and cocoa, coffee and pimento, cows and chickens, hopes and dreams. I drive the winding road, passing reams of people whose quality of life have been diminished by the unforgiving hands of the migration of many of our gifted friends and relations, unsympathetic politicians and larceny. Where have all the flowers gone?

In Jamaica, Chinese people developed the tradition of "the Shop" or the "Chiney Shop," where customers could buy small amounts of grocery items. This convenience certainly helped and at the same time exploited families on limited incomes and perpetuated the tradition of only buying just what was absolutely necessary for each meal—a few ounces of sugar, a quarter pound of flour, a half a pound of rice, a quarter pound of salt fish and even a slice of bread or a bulla. They also developed the concept of "trust" so accommodate customers who bought on credit. So the Chinese became culturally and affectionately known as the "Shopkeepers." While my father was one of these Shopkeepers, his departure out of our life when I was four years old was the last vestige of Chinese influence imprinted on me. I have visited China twice, had occasional relationships with people of Chinese heritage but no substantial oriental influence other than through reading. While I am aware that I look "Chinese," I have had an entirely "Black" experience and always worked for black organizations. So when I get "happy" as a Deacon in my Baptist church, it is something to behold. Notwithstanding the lack of Chinese influence, I nevertheless became a shop keeper.

Woodlands District was and is a 100 percent black community with various hues. They were all huemen except for two half Chiney Picknies who felt loved and cared for by all the people. The entire village raised us. I often say that during my childhood years, even though there were no police or any semblance of law enforcement, I never knew anyone who wanted to harm me or to be even impolite. There was no crime. Yes, I had four fist fights during my childhood, probably for being called "Chiney Nyam dawg," (37) but we were the best of friends a day later. I do not believe there is a better place in the universe to raise children than in a community in which every child has "mothers, fathers, cousins, aunties and uncles" throughout the community who were not blood relatives. "Good mawnin Mass Bertie. Respect to you sah."

Each generation of Chinese were able to obtain loans that were not available to other Jamaicans to start a Chinese Shop in another village after serving as apprentices in their father's shop and continue to expand their operations. They could never run out of villages to exploit. As there were no Chinese in Woodlands, someone had to keep shop. So it fell to Uncle Claudie. He started a small shop that became and remained successful throughout his lifetime. It died when his sons and daughters migrated to 'merica and they rented out the shop space.

Based on the Jamaican Chinese model, this one storey building had a main shop with three counters with a window at the end of each counter. The one to the right sold salt pork, salt fish, red herring, and salt mackerel. The centre sold asham (parched ground corn and sugar) sugar, salt, flour, bread, crackers, bullas, canned, and other baked goods with the scale in the middle. The left counter sold dry goods. This included shoes, cloth, needles, threads and buttons from a large glass case.

In addition to selling grocery, we also bought pimento (cloves), coffee, corn, and beans that we would sell to buyers who came by trucks. The public space was reserved for dominoes, and talking politics and how Cleve Lewis, their representative to Parliament was stealing the eye out of their heads. I learned to play all these games as well as enjoy arguing the topic of the hour. If someone wanted a drink, he would visit the rum shop next door where a mento or rumba band played music on Saturday nights and where Mass Claudie would put out salted snacks to make people thirsty so they would buy more beer and white rum that was referred to as just "waters." As no one wanted to drink alone, the bartender was forever offered drinks compliments of the customers generosity. Mass Claudie and I would have a special rum bottle of water from which he poured his drinks so he would not get drunk. After each customer, I would wash the glasses in a pail of soapy water, rinse, wipe them with a towel and turn them upside down on one of several wooden pegs on a tray.

I was working in Uncle Claudie's shop buying, selling, and making change by the time I was ten years old. It was a unique experience making change with pounds, shilling and pence. The smallest denomination was a farthing (one quarter of a penny that could buy an ounce of salt). A quatie was one and a half pence and could buy a slice of bread or a bulla and a shilling could buy a loaf of bread with a bulla as a bratta as a little incentive to buy again. It was a good education. I felt very privileged and "Big up" working behind the counter. I developed great relationships with people like Bradda Ashley Black, who taught me to drink gin and salt while we explored the mysteries of the universe and the great questions of life such as how Noah and his family handled all the shit the animals produced.

Occasionally, the "Iceman" who was also known as "Spirit" would bring blocks of ice from the ice factory in Santa Cruz (twenty miles away), transporting it in hampers covered with sawdust and walked behind his donkey back to Woodlands. He then converted it into ice cream (either run and raisin or grape nut), fresco (milk shake) as well as snow cones (shaved ice with strawberry syrup). These were wonderful treats and very refreshing!

My favorite treat at the time was Jell-O. I would give money to the truck driver who took people to Town to bring me a pack of strawberry Jell-O mix. I would have to wait until "Spirit" had ice. I would then mix the Jell-O in an Ovaltine can (one cup boiling water and one cup cold water) and place the precious liquid on the side of the ice to jell. I would impatiently check it regularly until I could enjoy the cool jelly slide down my throat. When I went "farrin" (38), my mother found out that I loved Jell-O and served it at every meal. Within a month, I got clide (39) and could not stand to even see the stuff.

My Grandmother was courted by a gentleman named Busha Price who was always giving me money and delighted in teaching me to write and recite poetry. He would finish each of his poems with "Lord Cornwallis, knock'na dough, turtle aback." I had no idea what it meant, but it had a rhythm to it and could be called a "scat." Whenever he wanted to be alone with Granny, he would give us some money and send us to New Market or Springfield to buy something that Granny needed. We dutifully got out of the way for several hours. I didn't figure this out until twenty years later.

One of the suppliers that came to the shop was "Mr. Lazarus." He drove a station wagon full of stuff: shoes, needles and thread, buttons, thimbles, knives, forks, spoons, tools, plates, cups, etc. Uncle Claudie would buy these items and sell them back to the customers. Mr. Lazarus was five feet tall and three hundred pounds. He would bet that the circumference of his waist was more than his height. Someone would always take the bet and lose. He is fond of saying "I am not deep, but I am very wide. It takes a long time to walk around me."

Uncle Claudie's filing system was a long nail that kept all his bills and receipts in perfect sequential order except that they all had a hole in the middle. Over the years, I adopted the same filing system even in this age of electronic filing. My secretaries and assistants always marveled that I could always find my messages and communications "filed" neatly on several message nails under my desk. No amount of encouragement on the part of my assistants or my wife could convince me to not use my trusty nail message holders. Old habits die hard.

The other habit that my wife objected to but later gave in to due to my persistence is hanging my clothes on nails. Growing up, there were no closets, so I had a nail for school clothes, one for church clothes and one for yard clothes. While I now have fancy hooks and lots of closet space, it just seems natural to hang some of my clothes or hooks instead of on hangers in a closet.

In our downtime and after closing the shop, we wrapped rice, corn meal, sugar, flour, poured coconut oil in "aerated wata" (40) bottles. I enjoyed making the black pepper funnels. We would also stock the shelves, sweep the floor, wash the glasses and wipe off the counter. While I was not paid for my work, I could eat all the candy I wanted and drink champagne cola (41). I even occasionally got permission to eat a can of sardines, bully beef or salmon which were wonderful treats. For the thirsty, I would pick a sour orange from a tree at the back of the shop and make lemonade or just mix strawberry syrup and water or condensed milk and water. To make extra money, I would buy a pound of sugar, cut up a coconut into little squares, and boil them together with a little ginger and sell each of these as "coconut drops" for thrupence. Each time I did this, I doubled my investment.

I learned about the dangers of drinking over-proof white rum first hand. Uncle Claudie always added water to the cast of over-proof rum that was bought directly from Appleton Estate so that people would not kill themselves. A boastful man actually took a bet that he could drink an entire bottle. He passed out and slept for a long time after he drank about a half bottle. I don't think he was ever the same after that. He was a ruined man.

The shop also sold kerosene aile (oil) to feed all the "Home Sweet Home" lamps in every household. Every so often, someone would knock one over and their entire house would go up in flames as the broken lamp would become a Molotov cocktail.

One Saturday nights when everyone was happy, I was dancing, and someone picked me up and put me on the counter so everyone could see how the Chiney Pickney could "wine up im waist." They all stopped dancing and I was the center of attention. They then had a good laugh, applauded, and gave me money. I was a professional dancer!

The store was open six days per week but only the side window was open on Sunday mornings because there was not supposed to be any work or business activity on our day of rest. Everyone (except Uncle Claudie) went to church.

For several years, The McDonalds' living quarters was in the back of the shop with a separate building for the kitchen and a latrine further away. I lived with my granny up the hill. As Mass Claudie amassed his fortune, he built a fine house on the hill overlooking the shop.

When I was twelve years old, Uncle Claudie decided to leave Aunt Myra and Uncle Ronnie (The Jew Boy) in charge of the shop in Woodlands and expand his operations to Springfield, about five miles away. He took this step even though Harry Chen-See ran a much larger shop up the street and Mr. Lynn Salmon and Miss. Zippy owned a similar shop on the other end of the village. The Chen Sees even had a gasoline pump where the attendant would measure out each gallon in a glass container on top of the pump before transferring it to the car. Miss. Ada and Miss. Gloria (mother and daughter) were particularly kind to me and even invited me to spend time with them behind the counter. I loved going to the bakery and fashioning animals with the bread dough and was delighted to take these handmade breads to Granny and my brother. I also remember that the Chen Sees raised turtles in a barrel for turtle soup. The post office was upstairs and across the street where I went to collect the boxes of "breguede" that my mother frequently sent.

I lived with Uncle Claudie at this new location for six days per week to help with the shop and keep his company. After we closed the shop on Saturday evening at 9:00 p.m., we would get on his high horse and ride the two and a half miles back to Woodlands with all his money in a bag. On other occasions, I loved riding Uncle Claudie's horse and even had a donkey that I sometimes rode to school.

Eventually, Uncle Claudie sold the Springfield shop and consolidated his business back to Woodlands, building a new shop that included space for the district postal agency.

On one of my trips to the big city of New Market, I asked Mr. Cummings, the Chinese owner of Cummings Dry Goods to give me a job as I now had plenty of experience as a shopkeeper. He immediately hired me. On Saturdays and holidays, I either took the "Champion Bus" or walked the five miles to and from work and earned real spending money. While in New Market, I made friends with Miss Maudie, a single Chinese lady, who owned a similar shop across the street.

I left Jamaica on April 5, 1959, and returned fifty years later to discover my beloved island all over again. I continue to believe in the old values and will continue to support the country of my birth and the people who nurtured me. This is "home" to my soul as I continue my Jamaica Chapter, hopefully participating in its past, present, and future.

CHAPTER I

Garnett's Broughupsy

The mau mau uprising was at its climax in Kenya, Gen. Dwight D. Eisenhower had been president of United States for nine months and Her Majesty Queen Mary had died six months earlier when Garnett Myrie came out of his muma, made his appearance and let out his first living cry on 27 September 1953. Both his mother and father's skin were as black as midnight. So Miss Minnet drank large amounts of cerese tea (42) throughout her pregnancy to assure a "browning," but he came out the same color as his parents.

He was born at home assisted by a nurse midwife. When he was born, as was the family tradition, his father entered the room, lifted up the child and proclaimed in a loud commanding voice "Bones of my bones, flesh of my flesh. Welcome! You shall be called Garnett Lloyd Myrie." Patrick, the older brother then accompanied his father out of the room with the baby's navel string and afterbirth that they buried under a young breadfruit tree to give the boy roots in the community while their mother dutifully counted his fingers and toes. It surprised her to find that he had already sprouted four teeth.

From his mother's perspective, Garnett seemed to take vindictive pleasure at her sudden jumps, winces, and exclamations in response to his bites at feeding time. Miss Minnet would swear to whoever was in earshot that she saw him smile after each feeding. And as he grew up, each time she overheard his "biting" remarks, she would be reminded of her tortured breasts. As an infant, his cries were so loud and demanding that those who heard him commented that he was trying to wake the dead when he wanted food or when his nappies were soiled.

He grew up the middle son of rural country parents for whom poverty and hardship were incentives to work hard so their sons would have a better life. His mother planted the "provision ground" (43) while his father, Nyrie, specialized in making beautiful mahoe and mahogany furniture. The smell of cedar, glue, and varnish permeated the shop and for about a mile in each direction. His father was also famous for his guitar playing every Saturday night with the "Herbie Arnold Rumba Band" when all the people, young and old, rich or poor alike would gather to dance, eat curry goat and rice, drink white rum, and make merry until midnight. The music stopped precisely at midnight so everyone would be ready for "chuch" come Sunday morning. The people were simple country folk, neither learned or wise. They went about their daily routines, eating, working, sleeping, praying, and singing with a peace that passeth all understanding.

Garnett Myrie got his broughtupsy in Woodlands District in Jamaica, a two hundred house village nestled in the rolling hills of St. Elizabeth. There he attended Springfield All Age Elementary School. Within the walls of this one-room school house, he was required to study the history of England as well as other incomprehensible stories from preindependence Jamaica. The imperial powers were determined to erase any thought of Africa replacing "Mother Africa" with "Mother England." So Garnett could recite the names of all the kings and queens of England as well as the wives of Henry VIII but was never schooled on anything African or Jamaican. He was asked to commit to memory Bible passages and poems by English poets and regurgitate them to the teacher with his classmates as eavesdroppers and spectators. With all the limitations of this fractured education, he nevertheless learned to read, write, and do arithmetic. But his great talent was to tell lies, which he did with creativity, conviction, and eloquence. Though he was not vindictive, he could embellish a story like no one else. Why tell the truth when it was just easier to lie? By the time he was twelve years old, lying became an engrained habit.

His lies were like a sport, and the good people of Woodlands half-jokingly called him a "liad." (44) The story of the boy who repeatedly cried "wolf" did not apply to Garnett because no matter how many times he lied, the people still believed his next lie. "But I really mean it this time! Its truth mi a tell yu." He was a genius at telling lies and persuading people that he was telling the truth.

For someone who never kept a promise or paid a debt, he had no difficulty borrowing money from acquaintances. He once borrowed ten shillings from his poor Uncle Humbedee, who loved the boy, even though five shillings would empty his pockets. Uncle Humbedee dutifully borrowed five more from someone else so he could loan Garnett the ten shillings he wanted. Lying was a skill he cultivated with great diligence once Garnett determined that only fools and children who had go to Sunday school told the truth. His father convinced him that growing up meant learning how to deceive. He became convinced that there were no such things as truths or facts but only versions. His penchant for lying was further fueled when he realized that people didn't want to hear the truth and preferred to hear lies. Women were always delighted to hear that they were pretty, particularly when they were not. Whenever he greeted a girl and even a young female teacher, he would ask them how they were and when they predictably answered "fine," his response was "Yes, you are!" and the women would be delighted to hear it and smiled back at him even though they thought he was "facey." (45) If he was in the mood, he would add, "Did you come down from Heaven? Are you an angel?"

But occasionally he found that the best way to convey misinformation was to tell the truth. When he truthfully told some of his acquaintances that he went to Black River where he saw the Ocean, three story buildings and paved roads, his reputation made his Comrades believe he was just showing off and both Sidney, Ronnie and Elton were more inclined to believe he only took a short trip to Springfield. Garnett was never sure if he was lying by telling the truth when he knew that his audience would believe the opposite. Ronnie said, "Mi hear sa yu a go a Springfield." His adversary believed he was lying as usual, and Garnett could not persuade the disbelievers. Later they would apologize for not believing him when Mass Clarlie, who was known for being a man of integrity and truth telling, told them that he and Garnett hopped a truck that took them to Black River. Unfortunately, they had to walk the twenty miles to get back. So Elton attempted to apologize, "Sorry fi wha mi did sa." Garnett would then delight in saying, "Hear mi now, we plant gungo together, and mi tell yu de truth but yu chat mi behind mi back and no believe me. Go whey. (46) Move yuself an siddung one side." Still, after great effort, he found more and more, that he couldn't fool all the people all the time. It frustrated him when he was genuinely trying to be truthful and wasn't believed as he couldn't always remember all the lies he told. As he grew older, it became more and more embarrassing and lying confused him as well.

Garnett also had a talent for cussing that he developed from listening intently to women who were verbally sparing and sometimes physically fighting over a man or when men were in verbal combat competing for the same woman or even when members of either sex felt disrespected. While Garnett was respectful enough not to utter bad words in the vicinity of a church or in the company of women, he frequently indulged in an orgy of forbidden words. He could string a large number of obscene words in one sentence that could kill a man at ten paces. His skill was also honed from his father who had the carpentry and cabinet-making business. Whenever the hammer hit one of his fingers, it was invariably followed by cussing. Garnett's orgy of forbidden Jamaican bad words were not limited to people either. When his pocketknife slipped while peeling sugar cane and cut his left thumb or when the machete slid off a "rock stone" and cut his left foot, two minutes of cussing the knife or the machete followed starting with "Jesus Christ, God Almighty." When a bird left droppings on his shirt after he was all dressed up for the dance, he directed two minutes of profanity in a vituperative attack on the inconsiderate bird who survived only because the poor creature had a wing and a prayer.

Early one Friday morning, he would learn a lesson in power when he sat on a wall watching Mr. Johntone Johnson and his helpers kill and prepare hogs for market. He asked the men if it didn't hurt the pigs when they stuck a knife into the animal's hearts and cut their throats. One of the butchers grabbed Garnett and the others joined in to hold him down as they put a knife to his throat. They asked a terrorized Garnett what he could do about it if they decided to butcher him. His struggles yielded nothing until the men decided to set him free. He immediately and literally ran for his life cussing as he went. Like his slave ancestors who lived and died on the sugar plantations nearby, he had learned the taste of fear and what it meant to be at the mercy of people who have complete power over others.

Woodlands children are strictly raised and are always on stage. Not only did they perform regularly in school and church plays but also under thatched roof makeshift halls and in homes, being asked to perform and show off what they learned at school. Whenever relatives and friends visited, they were enticed to recite poems, tell jokes, spell words, mimic the preacher, sing or dance. One of the important jobs that adults joyfully accepted was to encourage and big up the "yuths" (47) with a heap of praise. As a result, children grew up self-confident. Children were front and center of the community. Adults regularly beat them to keep them in line but children felt loved and cared for nevertheless. No child from Woodlands was without loving attention, but at the same time, people believed that children were born with the devil that had to be beaten out of them.

No history or map of Jamaica will include any reference to Woodlands but for those who know the place, it becomes part of their soul. The world may be ignorant of its existence but everyone here knows everyone else as well as who owns the many dogs, cows, goats, cats and even chickens. Social friendliness prevails. Two hundred little houses dot the mountainsides and the people live in peace and tranquility remote from the troubles of the world that they occasionally read about in week-old Gleaners that make their way to their village by those who had gone to "Town." They build their homes to enjoy the stately panorama but more importantly, to see approaching friend or foe in time to either run to greet them or flee.

The houses are covered with sheets of zinc. They love nothing more than snuggling in their beds in a rain storm. The romantic platter-platter is joy to their souls and food for men's libido. Whenever dark clouds gather overhead, Mr. Myrie would make his way home and head for their four-poster bed to snuggle down into their dried banana leaf mattress with his wife, even in the middle of the day.

Like other Woodlands people, the Myries are awakened by an orchestra each morning. The cock crows, the cat responds, the birds sing, the donkies bray, the cows moo and the goats bleep. They also retire from their day's labor with sunsets whose image linger long after dark, accompanied by a cacophony of the chirping of frogs, the tweet of insects, the occasional barking of dogs and the cool breeze rustling leaves.

The day begins early for women. From infancy to old age, from sun up to sun down, the women do most of the work. There is no job description or salary as they go about doing whatever needs to be done to promote the comfort and well-being of their families. Ms. Minnet carved out an existence on "mi piece of rockstone" by digging, planting, weeding, harvesting, preparing the meals, getting down on her knees to scrub and polish the floors with a coconut brush and beeswax with a rhythm that could serve as back-up for any reggae band, washing and ironing, sewing on the buttons, dawning the socks, mending the clothes, bearing children as well as carrying heavy burdens on her head on a catta (48) of banana leaves. It is sometimes a ten gallon tin of water brought from the parish tank or a large basket full of vegetables to market. She is not required to work more than sixteen hours per day except when her man needs her (which he does often).

The women of Woodlands District are "trong" and waste no time fretting about the yoke on their backs even when they are bent over, ached, racked with pain and become bruised. They will not even take an aspirin. While she is often bare footed, unacquainted with even the basic necessities of daily life and unadorned with fancy clothes and jewelry, the love and dedication she feels for her family and community is genuine, earnest, sincere, and occasionally enthusiastic, providing the wind beneath their wings and an umbrella when it rains. They use every opportunity to elevate the members of the community physically, morally, and spiritually—no one goes hungry. There is plenty of pain and suffering here, but it doesn't last. It just makes the joy of good times that much sweeter. Get to know any one of them, and you will find something to respect, something to admire and something to love. And when they reach the pearly gates of heaven, the angels will welcome them with songs of praise and God will utter the familiar words: "Well done, good and faithful servant. Come in and claim your reward."

If it wasn't for the women, the population would perish. They deserve to be cherished, offered encouragement, sympathy, love, and devotion. They get neither. They never ask what others can do for them, only the opportunity to be at service to one and all.

Other than issues relating to romance, the men of Woodlands are straight and honest and their dealings with his countrymen are fair. While all is fair in love and war, Mr. Nyrie Myrie's (Garnett's father) word was his bond in commerce. An honest day's work for an honest day's pay. Promises made were promises kept.

After the big men in the community went off to England, the young people were without guidance. In Africa, when young male elephants grow up without the influence of Alpha males they become unruly renegades.

Each morning, Garnett would see the remaining men making their way to "work their ground" an hour away wearing tattered clothes, water boots, a crocus bag over their right shoulder containing a pot, some salt pork to fry and flour to make dumplings for lunch in the bush. They don't eat salads or raw vegetables. On the left shoulder, they carry the tools of their trade, a pick axe, a fork and a hoe. In their right pocket, money and a knife. And in their left pocket, a handkerchief to wipe the sweat from their brow and to strain the water they drink from ponds. Out of these plots of land that sometimes contain more rocks than dirt, they bring home a harvest of carrots, corn, cabbage, scallions, tomatoes and peas (beans) that they sell in New Market, Montego Bay and Kingston. The Animals they raise are sold when school fees are due or to buy a major purchase like a radio that was powered by a car battery or a kerosene fueled refrigerator.

In addition to the Myrie's wooden tub, their other household furnishings included a panya jar with a thunder ball (53) to keep the drinking water cool. A two door cabinet with two drawers, five shelves and glass windows that displayed Mrs. Myrie's china, glasses, silver knives, folks, and spoons, but more importantly, that is where Garnett would find the condensed milk that he drank from time to time—straight out of the can.

In one corner of their dining room was a washstand made by Mr. Myrie where a porcelain basin sit in a circular space with a pitcher of water stationed under the basin with towels on both sides. A bar of Palmolive soap and a bottle of Detol is positioned beside the basin. No one is allowed to come to the table to eat before washing their hands and drying them off with the pretty towels embroidered with flowers that hung on the side of the washstand. As the doors and windows to their house were always open during the day, the chickens made themselves at home and went to any room they desired. A fowl even had the habit of laying eggs on Garnett's bed.

In the living room was a carved wooden sofa, a bench and a rocking chair for his Granny Zerefa. When company arrived, the three boys sit on the bench and listen to the conversation but they are never allowed to speak until spoken to. Children would respond to questions directly put to them or even perform a "kin pupa lick" (50) for the entertainment of their guests.

In the dining room was a long table with a bench for the children and four chairs for the adults where they shared wonderful meals. What was remarkable about the table, however, is that it was Garnett's pulpit. After Sunday dinner, his father would ask him to get up on the table and preach. In very exaggerated manners and voice, he would try to repeat what Parson had said at church. This was the source of great amusement for all who were present, and he just loved doing it.

Mrs. Myrie's joy came from talking on a veranda, on the side of the road, in the shade of a tree, leaning against a post, sitting down with a cup of tea or to accompany any meal. And when the curtains are drawn and the day shuts down, whispering sweet nothings after dark. Whenever there was a pause in the hussle and bussell of life, it was time to sit down with her frock folded between her knees or leaning on a post or wall visiting with a friend. Everyone in the community talk, tell jokes, tease each other and laugh, gesticulating with their hands, moving their heads up and down to agree and from side to side to disagree. They are a contentious people with strong opinions, and they make their points come alive using their entire bodies with exaggerated persuasive gestures. When they finish making their point, they would add for emphasis "END OF STORY. FULL STOP." (51)

They also win arguments by revealing that it was "written," and everyone knew that if it appears in the McDonald's Almanac, the Gleaner, or for that matter, if they could find a writing anywhere, it was accepted as fact. "Why would anyone write something if it wasn't true?" As they could offer little more, talking was the epitome of their pleasure. They love to gather and keep company. This sentiment was captured in the folk song "Long time now mi never see you, come mek wi walk and talk."(52)

Many women in Woodlands, in an effort to keep their shoes shinny and new would walk barefoot to church with their shoes knotted over their shoulders, wash their feet before fitting their feet back into these valuable pieces of leather. Ms. Gertrude would rejoice after cutting her foot on a sharp piece of glass bottle with an exclamation of gratitude that her shoes were in her hands as her foot would eventually heal but at least her shoes were not ruined. Not many of God's children had shoes in Woodlands.

Distances traveled by human feet were considerable. Riding a donkey, mule, horse or walking ten miles to Carmel Moravian Church for the Missionary Sunday Harvest Festival or three miles to New Market to shop was not taxing. The Champion Bus ran mornings and evenings but most people saved money by walking the distance talking and laughing in the company of friends and shouting pleasantries to neighbors or begging them for a cool glass of water as they passed. The one house that most people avoided belonged to the Obeahman who decorated his house with bones, flags of unknown origin, sticks and feathers organized for some symbolic purpose.

To light the way at night, travelers poured sixpence worth of kerosene in a bottle, stopped it up with a newspaper or cloth cork and set it on fire. When the light would go dim, the owner would be required to turn the bottle upside down to feed the fire. The sharp edge that cut Ms. Gertrude's foot came from one of these bottles that often lost their necks from the heat of the flame. Flashlights were in common use but these Molotov cocktails were cheaper than batteries.

Garnett could not help a smile whenever he witnessed the ceremony of men who poured out a little libation on the floor to the ancestors before throwing back the rum with one gulp accompanied with a hearty ahhhh and forcefully replacing the glass.

He could never erase the memory of the white dresses and headscarfs of the Pukkmania (53) and Kumina women and their vigorous singing, dancing and prancing accompanied with drums and homemade tambourines made out of bottle caps nailed to a bamboo frame. They struck fear in the community by making predictions about impending deaths and disasters, but Garnett was more amused seeing them falling to the ground convulsing as if in a trance.

Garnett enjoyed freely roaming the District in the company of his brothers and friends, swimming in ponds, climbing fruit trees in season, hunting birds with their catapults, playing marbles in every bare spot they could find, search for dead pimento trees that they would chop up with an axe and carry home to be used for fire wood—all without supervision of adults.

People readily and gleefully expressed love for each other. If a neighbor's cow was loose, someone would return it. If someone left clothes to "sun" and was not at home when it rained, a neighbor would rescue the clothes. They not only minded each other's business but took active responsibility for each other. Due to their nurturing and forgiving nature, the poor and needy were never neglected and sinners were always forgiven their transgressions. There was no expectation that anyone, except the parson and the Justice of the Peace would be perfect. "We are all dish rags in the sight of God."

For Nyrie and Minnet Myrie, their treasure was their three sons, youths verging on manhood. At eleven, twelve, and thirteen years old, while their father was an active part of their lives, the boys were obedient, never absent or even late for school, obeyed the teacher and diligently memorized their assigned Bible verses for Sunday school. All three boys helped their father in the cabinet shop sawing, planing and sanding boards, gluing and nailing as well as fitting joints. With encouragement from their mother, they also loved to grow things on the small farm the family owned. They faithfully planted their ground strictly with the advice of the "McDonalds Almanac" as well as with the waxing and waning of the moon. They all learned how to dig a yam hill, prepare the ground to sow carrot and cabbage seeds as well as plant cassava so they could make bammy (54) when the crop came in.

Garnett always had a patch of red peas that he called his cash crop. In addition to each boy owning and raising a goat kid, the boys also built a rabbit hutch and specialized in raising white rabbits which they fed the succulent Spanish needle that grew abundantly on the banks of the road. Selling rabbits meant they had money to buy cloth from Mass Claudie's shop that Ms.

Merri, the seamstress, would sew into school uniforms (blue shirt and brown kaki short pants). But mostly, he would say to his creditors, "Trust it to my account, on account that I don't have any money." He had a knack for cute sayings and was proud of himself whenever he came up with something that brought laughter to his audience.

In spite of a reputation for lying, Garnett remained a popular figure in the community because he was a jocular instigator, an inveterate trickster with an insatiable appetite for life. Whenever he left someone's company, he would say, "I'll see you when I look at you" or "See you later, alligator." There was always laughing going on whenever Garnett was around as everyone took turns being the butt of his jokes. He was always creating opportunities to laugh and play practical jokes on his trusting brothers and friends. His favorite trick was to hide and wait patiently in bushes and jumping out with a mighty roar at unsuspecting passersby. Nighttime was best. But they could not be angrier at him for these devilments than monkey could be angry at Anancy (55). He was the colorful, show off adventuresome son while his older brother Patrick and Joshie, the wash belly (youngest child), was quiet and unassuming who never developed the art of cussing.

Garnett was always talking, telling jokes, bragging, singing or whistling. His brothers would beg him to just shut up for a minute so a little peace and quiet could prevail. They would stop short of starting a fight as they knew that Garnett would never back down. Garnett would not give up until they were hurt and crying. When his brothers wanted something like clothes, money, a "sweetie" or anything else boys delighted in having or doing, they might get them, but if it was denied, they did without and did not complain. But Garnett would not stop pestering and insisting until he got what he wanted. Everyone obliged him so there would be peace in the house.

Whenever Woodlands people made the trip to New market, there was always a place when they had to decide to take the short cut or take the long road. The short cut meandered through private property and would require climbing walls. There was also the risk of aggressive bulls, dogs, and other dangers. If the owners of the properties saw them, it would also become contentious. One person would say, "Short cuts make long delays." Another would say: "long way draw sweat, short cuts draw blood." And even another would speak up in favor of taking the Mocho way by saying, "Taking too many short cuts produce failure while true success comes to those who take the right way." Garnett would always take the short cut and wondered why some people would choose to take the longer one. When the group divided, some taking the short cut and others taking the long route, he would say, "We will either beat you or see you when we get there."

Garnett was also rough with his clothes and the toys (gigs, marbles, go-carts, and sling shots) he made which didn't last long. So he ended up playing with his brother's kites, feefees (56) and balloons as well as wearing their clothes without permission and ruining them as well. Each morning, Garnett would use a tin cup of water that he dipped from the rain barrel to vigorously and loudly wash his face and gargle so everyone would hear but their mother had to ask his brothers if they had washed the sleep out of their eyes before she offered them a breakfast of hot milk and "cumback" (57) or an "Honest John" bulla.

His mother Minnet, and their granny Zerefa, both women of grace, were kind, loving, and forgiving women. Regardless of the persecutions others in the village heaped upon the three boys, they could rely on the comfort of abundant hugs and assurances of unconditional love at home.

Zerefa would wait for just the right opportunity to impart her wisdom to the children which often took the form of Jamaican sayings. She became concerned that Garnett was making too many enemies with his facey know it all attitude. So, one evening at supper, she said, "Every day you goad donkey, one day him will kick you." And then asked him, "Son, can one finger crack lice?" When he answered "no Granny" she then advised him that honey worked much better that vinegar to catch ants. "Make friends with everybody. Get people to want to help you if necessary. If you offend them, they will lay in wait for the opportunity to pay you back. That's just how people are. They get back at you. Now, if you get them on your side, while one finger may not be much of a weapon, fingers coming together as a fist is a weapon that can help you out a bad situation." Continuing on her finger analogies, she asked him to point a finger at her. "Now, look how many other fingers are pointing back at you. No one is perfect. So before you criticize the speck in someone else's eye. Take the log out of your own." As he was always respectful to his Granny, he merely replied, "Yes, Granny."

His father was much more direct and was often harsh, believing if he spared the rod, he would spoil the child, and they had to learn that life is hard for poor people. He often gave them licks for the most insignificant infractions. His father told the story of a man who was on his way to be hanged but as a final wish asked to speak to his father. As the father leaned over to listen to his son's last words, his son bit off the ear of his father, spit it out and then said: "If you had corrected me when I was a boy, I would not be put to death today." Garnett's father would end the story by proclaiming in a commanding voice: "No son of mine is going to bite off my ear!" So Garnett had mixed feelings when his Puppa left for England.

When Garnett gave Elton McFarlane a bloody nose in a fist fight after school, his victim limped home in a sorry state. The boy's angry father dragged Elton along to see Garnett's father about this wanton abuse. Nyrie called Garnett and cussed him shamefully in front of company and asked Garnett to go get a guava switch. With a panoply of insults heaped on the boy, his father ended with "I am going to beat the shit out of you and break your goddamn neck. Why can't you leave other people's pickney alone?" Elton's father, a peace-loving Elder at the Moravian Church who didn't believe in beating children, ended up pleading with Garnett's father not to beat Garnett and apologized for being a bother. "You know what, let's forget about it. Elton will be all right." Elton was hurriedly dragged by his father down the hill from the Myrie's house mumbling to his son, "What kind of people are these?" His only recourse was to urge his son to avoid Garnett as "him trouble."

The day after school closed at the end of the school year, Garnett climbed a tall star apple tree on Miss. Rosie's property and was enjoying the fruit's sweet creamy purple goodness when he saw his father and a single woman name Zethilda Parchment having sex behind the shop and watched with keen interest. A week later, Garnett saw the woman alone one night and after some small talk, told her what he had seen and said he would only keep it a secret if she did it with him as well. The shocked woman protested, "Oh my god! You are just a little boy!" To which he answered, "So?" She took him by the hand behind a wall and allowed him the same privilege as his father and made him promise afterward not to utter a word to anyone. "You promise?" She was the same age as his mother, and he was just half past twelve. He tried to ask her questions about what just happened but she just laughed at him and went home. Once it started, however, the "force ripe" (58) yuth could not stay away from the woman and found many other occasions to be alone with her sometimes at great risk of raising suspicion. She delighted in the attention of the boy and took the opportunity to teach him how to please her.

When the woman became pregnant, like many of the married men in the community, the elder Myrie proudly admitted his infidelity and confirmed that he had fathered the child and assumed support for his daughter. In a community where several of the big men had more than one family and most had outside children, the consequences were not severe and often made these men even more desirable to other women. In many instances, fatherhood meant only the act of donating sperm with no further thought of their responsibilities to the resulting children. Occasionally, however, women got into fierce fights over these men, and some of the women would become the laughing stock of the community.

Word came back from those who had migrated to England that jobs were available a plenty paying ten times what they made at home. So the Elder Myrie decided to go for a few years and save up enough money to expand his operations. Before departing for England, Nyrie made his rounds to bid farewell to all his neighbors who took turns wishing him well and blessing him. Teacher even reminded him that the streets of London were paved with gold so all that was required was for all a dem to bring back the gold. (Usain Bolt was to fulfill this prophecy in 2012)

Garnett was just a few months past his thirteenth birthday when his father bid him good bye. His liaisons with the Baby mother increased as she got comfortable with their unusual but consensual relationship. His excuse to his mother and the community for visiting her so often was that he wanted to play with the baby—his sister, as well as help the deserted woman with chores. Something always needed to be fixed.

Garnett had extended quarrels with his own mother about him being away from home so much as well as what deserved respect. He would accuse her of misplaced reverence to the Queen, and she would insist that "everybody knows that nutten black no good." In fact, she did not value anything Jamaican and always insisted on modeling her conduct on the ways of the old slave masters as well as only buying things (pots, silverware, clothes and can goods) made in Europe and 'merica. "If you want to make a life for yourself, you must leave this godforsaken country and go a foreign like yu puppa. Jamaica is hopeless hell, mi tell yu!" Garnett wondered to himself how he could disturb the sleep of the people from Woodlands so they could love themselves and not so focused on loving everything and everybody foreign.

By the time he was sixteen, both his parents had gone off to England. The migration of all the able bodied people from Woodlands District in search of employment in England was to have a devastating impact on the community. Starting in 1957, people sold their land to the owner of the Chinee Shop who made huge profits from these desperation sales. Just about all the young men and women went off to Britain, taking with them, the cricket club, the domino club, the gun club and even the ping-pong club. This mass migration took the life out of the community as well as the knowledge and skill required to train and shoe horses and mules. The leather-tanning operation closed down leaving only the cement troths behind that now collected water for cows and a mosquito haven. Suddenly, those left behind from the great migration had a hard time just getting four men together to play dominoes, have a drink with friends. Everything became dead, dead, dead.

Several couples pooled their resources to send the man off to make the way for a better life but on several occasions, loneliness got the best of them, and they took on other partners. When Uncle Ceryl was reminded in England that his wife was waiting for him to send for her, he would respond, "When I am not wid the one mi love, mi love the one mi wid." When Mass James came back after two years, he found another man living in his house and took his place as both husband and father to his children even though he had been regularly sending money to support them. No one had pulled his coat tail or schooled him about what was going on. Mass James got into a vicious fist fight with the intruder but gave up on reclaiming his family and went back to England to his other family. These extended absences and separations invariably lead to severe disruption in family life leading to domestic violence and even murder.

England's gain was certainly Jamaica's loss as the best teachers, the church organist, most of the church choir, the mason, rope-maker, shoemaker, the corn man, the carpenter, the barber, the tailor, the tobacco, and cigar man, the wet sugar man; and most regrettably, all the members of the "Herbie Arnold Rumba Band," including Nyrie Myrie, the guitar man, all went off to build up England after World War II. Back in Woodlands District, there was no one to play the magnificent church organ and no more live music was heard, no cricket matches, horse racing, picnics, Jankonoo parades (59) or lively Saturday night dances—only grandparents and children were left behind. Boys lost the mentorship of men, the skilled workers were gone and girls had fewer role models and little or no supervision—all were now dependent on remittances from England which did little to overcome the loneliness and boredom left behind.

Racism, the incessant rain, and the freezing cold in winter got the best of Brother Kirlew, the banjo player. So he gathered up everything he accumulated in England after two years and returned to Woodlands. He delighted in visiting the many women who were left behind and was frequently invited to lick the banjo while the women danced themselves into a frenzy. He was the popular guest in many homes until he settled down with Ms Mavis, the dressmaker, to father three more children for a total of eight.

On a Saturday afternoon, a week before the start of school in 1967 (just after his fourteenth birthday), Garnett was on his way back from Springfield. When he reached the Nurse's cottage, he saw the most beautiful girl he had ever seen. Unlike the long dresses that were the community standard, her likkle skirt was short, short, short. He immediately became aroused by her thighs and gasped with delight. What was this girl doing in Springfield?

So, he shouted across her gate, "Wha guan?" To his surprise she waved with the hand holding the soursop juice and came toward the gate. Being displaced, in her lonliness, she was only too anxious to meet someone her age. "I am Evadne—Nurse Woods is mi Auntie. She went off to deliver a baby a few hours ago and probably won't be back for a long time. My mother thought it would be best for me to attend school in the country as she claims I was too hard to control in Kingston. I just came down yesterday." "I am Garnett. Welcome to Country. I never met a girl from Town before, what is it like up there?" "Oh, we go to movies, parties and have a lot of fun. We dance a lot." Having said that, she snapped her finger, hummed a little tune as she did a little wind with her hips. So this is how the bad boy from country met the bad girl from town.

After some small talk, she decided to get down to business. "Do you know how to french kiss?" While he hesitated to admit his ignorance, he said no. "Well, come inside and let me show you." As she closed the door behind him, she placed her hands behind his neck, closed her eyes, and kissed him. He was dizzy with excitement and adolescent heat. "That's how they kiss in France," she announced. "Mi like it, you know. Show me again?" She didn't need much encouragement as she repeated the performance, but this time it lasted much longer. She set him on fire. She told him to go quickly before her Auntie came home. If you want to do it again, you have fi wait till she go deliver another baby. "Nice meeting you Garnett." "Nice meeting you too." He left her feeling like the "force ripe man" he had become.

He became obsessed. He hid in the bushes by her house waiting for Nurse to be called. When she was called, she saddled her horse, took her doctor bag, and went off to bring a new life into the world. He timed it perfectly and knocked on the back door. Within seconds, they were in sweet embrace practicing to become French citizens.

When school started, he couldn't help smiling and admiring Evadne but pretended they had just met. He pretended indifference but she was never out of his mind or his fantasies. He was obliged to spend most of his free time with Carolyn who had rules about what they could do but whenever the opportunity presented itself, he and Evadne would be doing it over and over and over again pausing occasionally to discuss life issues. One of the insights she shared was: "In Kingston, everything is allowed except what is specifically forbidden. In the country, everything is forbidden except what is allowed. In Kingston, everything is hopeless but not serious. In country everything is serious but not hopeless."

As his erotic attachment took hold, he was willing to spend many hours behind the wall at the cemetery hoping that Nurse Woods would be called away. More often than not, however, he would wait all day with some fruit that he had brought for his love but ending up eating them himself as he became famished. When no babies required Nurse Woods services, she stayed comfortably at home. He would eventually give up after a long wait to return another day.

But some days he got lucky. He would see Nurse on her high horse going to a delivery and made his way to Evadne's arms where they laughed, talked, danced, and of course indulged in a great variety of delights.

It was not to last, however, as just before Christmas, Evadne would become pregnant, and she was sent back to Kingston. The very thing that her mother and Auntie were trying to avoid by sending her to country came true. Her Auntie sent her back to Kingston, and regrettably, the pretty young gal from town vanished from his life.

In the months that followed his father's migration to England, while the other children at school were being obedient, Garnett began his resistance. The "Likkle" yuth became a rude boy. While some embraced the rebellious attitude of the yuth, others rejected him for carrying on so bad.

In an attempt to crush his spirit, he was severely and repeatedly beaten by his teachers, several other adults in the community as well as his mother, but he was like cork. No matter how many times they tried to keep him down, he would float up again. Some said he had his name on teacher's strap, as Teacher Ferguson, a stern unsmiling man, who hated precocious students, took vindictive pleasure beating him. On the other hand, Garnett was born mischievous, defied authority, and could never stop punching the boy who sat to his right or pulling the hair of the girl who sat in front of him. He had a natural tendency to get into trouble, so he occupied a great deal of the teacher's attention. When the head teacher started to beat him, he would cry out as "eye water" well up and finally overflow their banks and trickled down his cheeks. Occasionally, when it was bedtime and he removed his clothes, the blood from these abrasions would be caked to his shirt. Although his mother was sympathetic, she did not dare register any objections but instead urged her son to be more obedient. "Behave nuh man?"

Eventually, he got used to being treated harshly, became fearless and refused to cry out in pain. He would rub cow-itch (Mucuna pruriens) and scallion on his palm to deaden the skin whenever he thought he was to get a beating, but he was no longer afraid of pain. Unfortunately, he occasionally forgot that he was handling cow itch and inadvertently rubbed his eyes with his fingers or he took out his penis to pee. This simple act would lead to several hours of enormous suffering as washing with soap and water did not help.

Sometimes, Teacher Ferguson grew weary before a tear was shed and the shock of the hits would eventually diminish. When teacher ended the beating, Garnett would bite his trembling lower lip, fiercely look straight into teacher's eyes, gritted his teeth and continued to put out his hand asking for more or he would defiantly ask, "Is that all you got?" Sometimes it was a guava switch or bamboo cane to his backside while he was touching his toes in front of the whole school, sometimes a belt, and sometimes, it was a store bought cowhide strap made especially for beating children and sold throughout Jamaica for these occasions. Garnett actually enjoyed showing off to the other "pickney dem" how much licking he could take, so he sometimes purposefully vexed the teacher. These episodes confounded his teachers and awed everyone else.

Woodlands people believed in the sanctity of the status quo and vigorously expressed themselves on every topic that came up while at the same time did not believe their opinion mattered to anyone else but themselves. So they continued to proudly display portraits of Queen Elizabeth II in their living rooms. Jamaica obtained its independence from England in 1962 when Garnett was ten years old and throughout the sixties, Garnett's life was varied and mostly pleasant but the rules against non-conformity were stringent and the penalties severe. As he became more and more impatient with people for not accepting the truths he discovered that he thought were self-evident, the more they felt disrespected. So he was beaten almost daily. This was not unusual for Woodlands boys, so he supposed that it was the correct thing teachers and the elders of the community were supposed to do.

The pain he could not tolerate when he was thirteen, however, was a toothache. He complained of a toothache for a week and increasingly cried out in agony and became dizzy with pain but all his mother could offer were cotton balls soaked in bay rum on the impacted tooth, willow bark and ganja tea as well as a hot towel wrapped around his head which she sympathetically placed on her lap, while encouraging him to sleep. He would have to wait until the following Thursday when Dentist Wiggins was due to visit Woodlands. In the meantime, he was worn out with the intense pain that kept the entire household awake. He loudly cried out as the exposed nerves in the tooth tortured him.

Finally, Dentist Wiggins arrived, as Novocain was not available, after a drink of over-proof white rum, two men volunteered to hold him down with his head back while Dentist Wiggins pulled the decayed tooth. He bled profusely in the basin next to him and slept for the rest of the day and through the following night. The pain was gone, and while his mouth was sore for a few more days, he rinsed with saltwater three times per day, and he was soon back to his old self. He thought he had learned a lesson about having to die before going to heaven. Then he wondered if he could make himself appreciate being able to see, without first being blind. Even though he was never blind, he shouted out, "I can see! I can see! I can see!" It felt good to him, and he laughed to himself.

When Garnett was approaching his fourteenth birthday, he got a fever, chills, and a cough. His grandmother said, "The pickney burning up with fever." She dipped rainwater that had run off the zinc roof and travelled along the gutters made from split bamboo and filled the drum at the edge of the house. She balanced the cleaned out ten gallon kerosene can full of water on three rock stones over a raging wood fire and after the air bubbles broke the surface, poured it into their wooden tub with some lemon (fever) grass. She made a seat for him by placing a slab of lumber across the middle of the tub and told the boy to sit naked on the slab with his feet outside the tub as the water hot. She gave him a cup of bush tea (60), covered him with two blankets. For the next hour, he sipped on ganja tea and sweated. There was so much perspiration that he thought the water level increased a full inch from the output from his body. He emerged with his fever broken and according to his grandmother. "His conscience is now clear and all his sins have been washed away. All the corruption gone." He then had a good night's sleep dreaming that he was flying like a bird and would start up his shenanigans again the next day.

The Easter play at church cast Garnett in the role of the Centurion and Teacher Ferguson as Jesus. When it came time for the Centurion to slap Jesus and tell him to shut up, Garnett couldn't help himself and, in an act of sweet revenge, gave teacher a hard slap in the face. And while he would have won an Oscar for the convincing performance, teacher, as well as the entire audience, was shocked, and gasped in horror. The gasp created a pregnant pause, but as the show had to go on, teacher got over it and decided not to seek redress. But Garnett scored lots of points from his school mates who wished they had enough courage to do such an outrageous thing.

Garnett was not a criminal by nature but circumstances changed him. Stealing cane, mangoes, neaseberries, grapefruit, oranges, tangerines, plums and gineps from neighbors was not considered stealing. All the "pickney dem" from the district enjoyed this privilege. Once, while clearing land to plant corn, he saw one of Ms. Rosie's fowls coming from a hiding place, and discovered a nest with six brown eggs. He picked them up and sold them to the local shop for two shillings and bought bullas (cookies) and Cola Champaign with the proceeds which he shared with his brothers who then told their mother. She confronted him leading to a confession but complained bitterly to his brothers that "no good deed every goes unpunished." If he had not shared his bullas no one would have been the wiser. The neighbor was compensated and Garnett, shamefaced, held his eyes to the ground while apologizing to Miss Rosie.

With a special request from his Grandmother, the owners of the "Chinee" shop (grocery store) in the District hired Garnett as the yard boy to chop bush, keep their yard clean, tend to the small home garden and do other handyman-type work as needed. For this they paid him a pittance—a shilling a day. His devouring ambition had him set his sights on much bigger things in life and the lack of money was like a great wall to his ambitions.

He often observed the shop owner and his wife bringing each day's take in a small grip (cashbox) up to the house each evening after closing. So he set his sights on stealing the grip and making his escape. One evening, as the sun was going down, Garnett had the gumption to quietly make his way into the shop owner's bedroom and hid under the bed. This was not difficult as the doors to the house were never locked, and as a trusted employee, Garnett had ample access to the house. He didn't want to hurt anyone, just to grab the grip when the occupants of the house fell asleep and quietly make his escape. He reasoned that the shop owners were so rich, they wouldn't even miss that little bit of money, and it would give Garnett a start on his road to prosperity.

While he laid quietly under the bed for several hours, he daydreamed of being a "Big Man" with his own house, a horse and a car. He would show them. One day, he would enjoy the envy of the entire community and have his way with any woman he desired. The thought made him smile. He closed his eyes and pretended that it was all real to him—especially riding around the village on the back of his white horse and wide-brimmed hat waving to his admiring subjects.

When the shopkeepers arrived home that fateful evening, they placed the grip conspicuously on their bureau, washed up, changed into their night clothes and went to bed. When Mass Harry heard snoring, he "jucked" (61) his wife and asked if she was already asleep as he was in the mood. She responded, "It no me!" Whereupon they realized that someone was sleeping under their bed. Poor Garnett never anticipated that he would fall asleep if he lay under the bed with nothing to do for several hours and was now snoring loudly.

The man ran for the broom and repeatedly hit Garnett and yelled as loud as he could, "Tief! Tief! Tief!" Mass Harry yelled out some bad words and aggressively ran Garnett out of their house. The ruckus woke everyone in this sleepy village and Garnett, suffering the agony of his lacerated conscience, ran away in disgrace.

He had no opportunity to prepare for his adventure and left barefoot with only the clothes on his back. Fortunately, it was a full moon. He was in the bush all by himself alone in the middle of the night, and he felt afraid. For the first time in his life, he had no one to talk to or harass. He reflected on Teacher Ferguson telling the class that other than mongoose and wild hogs, Jamaica had no wild or dangerous animals but every duppy story he ever heard came back to him. He told himself that duppies were not real but in his situation, he was not so sure. As he gathered up some leaves to make a bed, he cried. As he tried to catch a sleep, every strange sound he heard startled him. The day before, he had had dreams of being a hero but for now he only wanted to survive the night, expecting to be awakened by the District Constable, put in handcuffs and lead off to prison. He was an outlaw.

Garnett's grandmother, who was on friendly terms with the shop owners, begged them to forgive Garnett which they agreed to do as nothing was stolen but Garnett didn't know about these negotiations and was afraid and decided to "hide a bush" washing in ponds and eating fruits and berries. It was mango season, so he had no trouble keeping his belly full with these esculent fruit. Even though he was lost in the woods, he got used to his situation and now considered himself a "Rootsman" or an escaped slave who could survive anything. Later when he was a soldier in Africa, he would remember the lessons he learned surviving alone in the bush.

In his wanderings for two days, he bucked upon the man they called "Little Man" tending to his ganja plants beside a pond over in Tenancy Mountain and Garnett feeling compelled to have human contact, yelled out, "Wha guan sa?" Not expecting anyone, Little Man was startled and looked around to where the voice came from and found Garnett up a tree. "Hay man, everybody talking about you! How yu do?" "Mi getting along." After helping to weed around the fifty or so ganja plants, Little Man offered him a cartwheel dumpling with fried pork served on a coco leaf as well as some hard dough bread and lemonade made with sour oranges and wet sugar. Little Man then took out a spliff, and they took turns smoking and getting high. "That's some good shit you have Little Man." As their chance encounter wound down, he asked Little Man for the box of matches so he could make a fire. The meeting reminded Garnett of home, and he felt sad but returned to the bush and asked Little Man not to tell anyone. But of course, this was news Little Man found impossible to keep to himself.

On the third day of his isolation, he was enjoying the cool breeze sitting with his back against a mango tree. He had just eaten his belly full of mangoes and was dozing off and trying to decide if he should go for a swim in the nearby pond when he heard his brothers calling out his name. Garnett was never so happy to hear his brother's voices that he got up immediately and started running toward the voices but was quickly overcome by his urge to play a trick on them. He turned back and climbed the mango tree and stayed hidden from them. His brothers approached and noticed the freshly discarded mango skins and seeds and decided that he must be there abouts. Patrick said, "Somebody nam dem belly full and gone a rass!" As if an invitation was extended, Garnett jumped from the mango tree with a blood curdling yell. His brothers jumped back but quickly recognized Garnett. They hugged and sat down to talk.

They informed him that he was forgiven for his crime and his mother and grandmother were anxious to have him back home. They told him that no one was angry but were definitely laughing about the incident. This news did not make him feel any better. He nevertheless got up enough courage to accompany his brothers out of the woods and back home. He was expecting the worse but to his surprise, his brothers as well as his mother were glad to see him back home like the story in the Bible about the Prodigal son. In her joy, his Granny hugged up on him like she never did before. While it was not the fatted calf, he was treated to curry chicken and rice as well as a proper bath. His mother was particularly glad that he was safe and decided not to punish him.

In the following weeks, the people in the community would snore loudly in his presence and laughed at his folly. The entire affair embarrassed him to no end. He roamed the village decidedly humbled and without his usual bravado. He even went to the shop keeper to ask forgiveness. Mass Harry didn't give him his job back but let him get away with a lecture and shook hands to assure him that all was forgiven due to his yuth. He did warn him that serious trouble was ahead if he didn't change his ways. The shopkeeper said to him, "Listen to me, if Christmas wasn't coming, I would bring up the police from New Market, and you would be in jail right now, and once you have a prison record, you will never be allowed to go to high school, get a visa to visit another country or get a job. I only beg you to learn from this experience. I hope what mi tell yu will not fall on deaf ears. A life of crime only take you to one of two places, the grave or prison." His only response was "Tank yu sah." The boy could be humble.

As soon as the Christmas breeze began to blow, the boys busied themselves chopping the grass in their yard with a sharp machete and white washing the big stones that they placed six feet apart lining the walkway all the way from the main road right up to the house steps. They even white washed trunks of trees in the yard and brought in blood red poinsettias that grew in the yard to put on the dining table.

Aunt Beryl Burchell came in from Kingston along with other relatives so the children had to sleep on the floor but they didn't mind with all the festivities at hand. Everyone was hugging up on each other and laughing, eating ham and roast beef, and drinking sorrel and Guinness stout. While Zerefa was in charge of the cooking, she was also busy sending someone to buy what she needed for their meals at Claudie's shop, firewood to stoke the fire, someone to get water from up tank, someone else to peel the yam, sweet potatoes and sweet cassava. There were always dishes to wash. The three boys, now thirteen, fourteen and fifteen, were kept busy but as usual, Garnett could ginal his brothers to do most of his chores.

Aunt Beryl asked the children to recite poetry and Bible verses, sing songs and even dance to music from the gramophone she brought with her. While Patrick and Joshie were shy, Garnett excelled and showed off in everything he was asked to do. When he was asked how he learned to do Kingston dances, he was tempted to tell her about Evadne but instead answered, "Mi just know!" Aunt Beryl joyfully encouraged and big up the boys with a heap of praise. They played the "Back to back, belly to belly" song over and over with the appropriate moves to the delight of their granny.

He watched as his Uncle Cephus soaped up his face and shaved holding a two-inch double-edged razor blade very gingerly with three fingers and looking at himself on the small mirror he cotched on the ackee tree in the yard. It was not a smooth shave as his uncle's face was bloody from the nicks left behind by the razor blade. When they went to Barber Warren to get their hair cut they had to wait under the eave of the shop and Taylor Cahoon would use the big iron with the red coals inside to crease their pants. All the boys got new shoes for Christmas and they were clean and shining for about an hour until the dust and mud from the road got them dirty again. The women in the house did each other's hair, and they were all dressed up in fancy crinoline dresses and awash with kuss kuss perfume. The girls also used coconut oil to shine up their legs. In their visits to the neighbors, they were offered fruit cake with coco tea and greeted everyone with "Happy Christmas" and the intended receiver of the greeting predictably added, "When it comes."

When the eagerly anticipated day arrived, the sky was robin egg blue and Christmas breeze was warm in the sunshine and cool in the shade. The boys woke up as soon as the day break out and the first cock crowed, got dressed, and yelled out almost in unison "Happy Christmas" with much anticipation and laughter. The entire community would become one choir singing. "Look at the bright morning star when the Gabriel angel come. Hip, hip after hurrah." Like drums in Africa, they immediately started with the fire crackers that were answered by the other people throughout the community. Garnett prided himself on being able to hold the fire crackers against his fingers without getting hurt when they exploded. Even though the sun was just rising and the cock had only crowed twice, choir members from the Moravian Church could be heard singing as they walked to the houses of those who were alone, sick or shut in to sing Christmas Carols and cheer them up.

Their attention then turned to Zerefa's Christmas egg punch. Garnett went over to the common to milk the cow. Zerefa took the milk from him and put it on the fire to scald, crack a dozen eggs and carefully separate the red (62) from the white and discarded the eye (63). She handed the bowl with the yolk and brown sugar to Garnett to grind and the whites with a few drops of water to Patrick to whip with a fork. When the yolk was nice and creamy and the white was fluffy, she combined them, added hot milk, a Guinness stout, and a Red Stripe Beer, grated nutmeg, vanilla extract, mixed it all up and served it for breakfast. After drinking the concoction, they all celebrated with the traditional and satisfying "Ahhhhhhhhhh." Everyone was now sporting a white mustache.

After breakfast, their mother gave the boys their Christmas money, and they headed out to the community picnic at Shield's Pon where vendors sold ice cream and fresco (milk shakes), grater cake, pound cake, jerk pork, fried fish, cane juice, peppermint sticks, and all the treats of Christmas. Aunt Beryl ate a little of everything and was heard to proclaim, "tings nice fi true u know!" Her sister's response was: "tru dat!"

Garnett did not know what a war was but some of the men who were veterans of both World War I and II (fighting with the British) marched around in ill-fitting uniforms and wooden rifles. They looked so boosey (64) that Garnett also pretended to be a soldier and delighted in marching every step with them.

The merry-go-round was built by the men in the community. The large logs bearing the four riders was reinforced by scaffolding and suspended on a hard plate where grease was applied regularly. The stronger men took turns turning the riders as fast as they could to the delight of both riders and lookers-on.

Everyone, young and old took a ribbon and danced around the colorful Maypole until their ribbons were plaited up, and then they danced again the other way around until it was free, and then they would plait it up all over again. Garnett always took the red ribbon. Everyone commented on how it was not the same without Herbie Arnold Rumba Band who had all migrated to England and Garnett missed his father and wished he could delight a crowd like his father did with his music. Now, those who were left behind had to sing the songs acapela. Nurse Woods tried to tell everyone that they didn't need music to have a good time but it was just a bluff. They really did miss the music. As the evening shodows got longer and longer, they felt exhausted but happy.

Aunt Beryl went back to Kingston on Boxing Day. As Most of the men were gone to England, no cricket match or horse racing was organized.

After their father left for England, it was Garnett, not his older "Breda" Patrick or younger Joshie who became the man of the house. He became the abandoned women's comfort, pride, and joy. His grandmother Zerefa prayed for Garnett daily and encouraged him to continue to attend Sunday school. He tried to comply just to please her but he was frustrated with the empty worship service, and he exasperated the Minister with incessant questions:

"How can God create something out of nothing?"

"What was God standing on when he created the universe?"

"Did Adam and Eve have navels?"

"I want my heaven on earth. Why do I have to wait until me dead?"

"How could a woman have a child without having sex with a man?"

"Is God a just god or a one-eyed god? How come him favor white people. Why black people always being in slavery and treated bad?"

"After Adam and Eve had Cain and Abel, who did the sons have pickney with?"

"How can a man survive in the belly of a fish?"

Minister's usual response was merely, "Son, with God, all things are possible. He will also even things out and remove all evil from your path if you just trust him and obey his commandments." Unlike the rest of the church members who revered and believed everything Minister said with blind affectionate obedience, Garnett was not satisfied with this answer. He didn't take telling. When Minister Todd quoted Mathew 6:14-15, "For if you forgive men when they sin against you, your heavenly father will also forgive you. But if you do not forgive men their sins, your father will not forgive your sins." He responded, "As nice as that sounds Pastor, mi can't do it and mi no wa fi do it. (65) An eye for an eye and a tooth for a tooth works for me. Englishmen discovered the cross by way of the Bible, black people discovered the Bible by way of the cross. I care for no one who doesn't care about me."

And the Parson's response was, "But that would leave the country toothless and blind." There is a great deal of injustice in the world but you invite more injustice if you don't forgive those who treat you unfairly. Violence and hostility does change the world. It makes the world more hostile and violent." With regard to his reputation for lying, Minister would just say, "Son, no truth is ugly, and no lie is beautiful." But he was not convinced as Garnett considered himself the consummate liar.

Minister would continue his counsel by advising Garnett to not confuse intolerance with steadfastness. "In this world, as you eat your fish, you must spit out the bones. You will never get everything the way you want it. That chip on your shoulder is going to get heavier and heavier as time goes on. Nobody is perfect, especially you. So if you want to live in peace and harmony with everyone, you have to start by accepting that we all have faults. More importantly, everybody does the best they can one hundred percent of the time. Regardless of how obscene, rude, wrong, unlawful, and insulting their behavior is, that is really all they are capable of being, given their genes, their upbringing, their environment, and all the things that influence their behavior. As a minister, I have to accept every person the way they are. I can hopefully bring about some positive changes but I start by accepting everyone—unconditionally. God does just that by loving us all just as we are. Then to add a full stop, Minister sang an old hymn to Garnett, "Just as I am without one plea . . . Just as I am, poor, wretched, blind; sight, riches, healing of the mind." For a moment, Garnett was humbled and was a little grateful for his time with minister.

While his mother was less attentive, his grandmother continued to dress her grandsons and send them off to Sunday school and when everyone in the community was darkening the steps of the church with eleven O'clock shadows in celebration of their sacred day of rest, Garnett was seen picking pimento and collecting tangerines from Mother Blake's property. Promising himself not to break the Sabbath more than once per week, he found numerous ways to show his disdain and would find ways to dishonor the Sabbath by drinking rum and smoking cigars and ganja in plain view. He had become oblivious to ridicule and didn't understand what the fuss was all about as his grandmother regularly made ganja tea for him when he was not feeling well.

While Garnett loved to sing hymns and see his comrades, he did not enjoy anything else, he just endured it. All three boys complied for a while and dutifully attended both Sunday school and church, but then Garnett started using the money his mother gave him for the collection plate to buy sweeties. He enjoyed everything Ms. Rose Chambers made: coconut drops, bus-mi-jaw bone (66) grater cakes and gizadas (67). He wanted to buy more. So he put in a penny and took out eleven pence from the collection plate pretending to make change for a shilling. A Steward in the Moravian Church caught him, slapped his hand and put him out of the church.

After a lonely walk home, he not only took the cream from the top of the milk in the pitcher and swallowed it in one gulp as well as drank the whole can of condensed milk that his mother had just opened that morning and made the satisfying ahhhh when he finished drinking something that hit the spot. He even remembered that his Granny told him that cream always rises to the top and smiled as he thought himself to be cream that could face any adversity.

After the benediction was song at church, everyone made their way home to feast on the traditional Sunday meal of browned stew chicken and rice and peas. The entire family then went to visit other families. No one decided who the visitors or the hosts were but the slightly better off people stayed home to receive others. It was a mini Christmas when special treats were shared, sweeties, cane juice as well as guava, sour sop, sweet sop or custard apple juice mixed with sweet milk with a drizzle of nutmeg, puddings and cakes with homemade ice cream. The boys took turns fitting the gears over the container with the creamy mixture, latching it down, breaking up the ice with an ice pick and packing it with coarse salt around the bucket. Then they turned the handle until it could turn no more. Aunt Dottie was then called to uncover the ice cream and give the pallet to her favorite nephew—Garnett. These are moments of sheer joy, and Garnett would grab the pallet and with others competing for this treat, run toward the mango tree licking the left over ice cream as he went, with others following after him. He often wished for an entire week of Sundays.

Each Sunday afternoon, the kindness of the people came alive in their most vigorous, engaging and generous states. Children skipped rope, played hop scotch and a multitude of games. The adults, sitting and talking on the verandah, delighted in the screams of sheer happiness coming from the children. It was also big fun when someone played some music and the adults watched the children wind up dem waist.

Interspersed among the fruit trees, every yard sported a flower garden in their front yard, a terrestrial paradise with ample supply of jasmine, hibiscus, roses, red ginger, bougainvillea, heliconia, zinnias, dahlias, anthuriums, lilies, marigolds and crouton that passersby stopped to admire and ask for a bud to make their own gardens even more beautiful. More often they would steal a sprig as they believed the plant was more likely to survive if it was stolen.

As dusk overcame daylight, people enjoyed each other's company so much it was difficult to bid "good night." Instead, they would walk each other home but then those who were home had to walk their guests home and so they would go back and forth several time before finally agreeing to part midway and make their own way home. This was the epitome of the Jamaican pleasure trips—walking and talking.

After they returned home from their Sunday visits, his mother picked up the empty condensed milk can and tried to pour out some of the sweet milk into her tea and shouted out her disappointment. Garnett lied and said he didn't know anything about it. Later that evening, he ate all the corn pone that was left except for a small piece that he offered to Patrick and so when the inevitable question was asked, "Who finished the pone?" His brother had to confess and got licks for it as his mother repeated with each lick, "When you want something, ask for it."

On Fridays (Butcher Day) Garnett's granny bought, cleaned and prepared the intestines (tripe) of cows and placed them on sticks high above the open fire in the kitchen to smoke and cure. The boys were forbidden to eat them without permission but they found a way to cut them without leaving evidence that they stole the tripe by using a hot knife that resealed the cut, and they would roast them in the hot coals using a stick to turn them and finally had a feast accompanied with hard dough bread or roast breadfruit. They joyfully wiped the fat that ran down the sides of their mouths with their hands, closed their eyes, licked their fingers and pulled up the sides of their mouths. These were special moments for the boys, and while they thought they were getting away with something, their granny knew all along what they were up to but did not deny them this joyful pleasure.

Garnett once stole the teacher's fountain pen but when the teacher was searching each student, Garnett slipped the pen into the pocket of Georgie Phillips who received six licks with the strap and a reputation as a thief when the pen was found. Poor Georgie could not tell the truth and even confessed that he took the pen as he knew Garnett would beat him up if he told on him.

After demonstrating his superior fist fighting, the other boys just gave him money without Garnett even having to ask them for it. His generosity with girls with the money he got from the other boys paid off as he could kiss just about any of them. They all wanted to be his friend even when their grand-parents (who were trying to raise them in the absence of their parents who went off to England), told them that Garnett was a bad boy and cautioned them to avoid him.

Their Mumma and Pupa's warning notwithstanding, several boys secretly admired him. He had both the talk and the walk. He even had two loyal lieutenants, Melvin and Ronnie, who liked the idea of being friends with the big man at school but were not necessarily happy when they were commanded to do his bidding, especially when it conflicted with their parent's wishes. Once they committed to their role as Garnett's assistants, however, they were no longer free and had to do his bidding and got more thumps and slaps than anyone else from Garnett who was now invested in keeping them in line.

He was respected by the remnant of men in the community that they invited him to walk and talk with them and so he got accustomed to the company of older men and learned a great deal from older women as well.

Everyone was committed to the sanctity of the status quo. Inasmuch as all the children were brought up to believe that bad things were supposed to happen to people who disobeyed or opposed their parents, the Justice of the Peace, the teachers, the minister and even God; they were at odds to explain how Garnett was not hit by lightning, had not gotten sick or were paid back for dramatically flaunting his sins. But nothing could hurt him. Uncle Bertie would complain, "So how come when mi do the least little thing wrong, mi get hurt and mi ground no bear? Where is the justice?" Garnett grew into an extremely attractive young man, a good fighter and a fast runner with a superb constitution. He remained in excellent health throughout his youth.

In 1967, when he was fourteen, his focus changed when his father's brother Humbedee went to 'merica to do farmwork brought back several books and records relating to the Black Power and Civil Rights movement that was taking hold in the United States. He loved his books and his records. He loved the James Brown song: "Say it loud, I am black and I am proud" that he played over and over again on his uncle's gramophone. When he sang along with James Brown, he felt emancipated and overcome with happiness. He was particularly taken with books about Stokely Carmichael, Malcolm X and Martin Luther King and was fond of memorizing their speeches. He thought the words in these books were eloquent. The resulting pride and elevated spirit he garnered from his books brought about a great love of reading. While he read and contemplated the idea that all men are equal, as much as he wanted to believe and subscribe to it, he couldn't bring himself to believe it. Could it be true that rich white people are equal to the poorest black man? How could a woman from Woodlands be equal to the Queen of England? All these things he contemplated in his heart.

Although most of these books were beyond his comprehension, they were the only reading materials available to him. As he struggled with the difficult vocabulary, it was an awakening for him and he not only grew up, he was now on a mission. While others his age were frittering away in frivolous amusement sucking their thumbs, twirling hula hoops, guiding bicycle tires with a wire bent around them, playing marbles, cooshue (cashew), checkers, hop scotch, dominoes, all fours and strip me naked (card games), the young Myrie tried very hard to learn his books and was enriching his mind with "Black Pride." He aspired to join the Black Panthers and was particularly drawn to Bobby Seals. He begged his cousin to bring back more books on his next assignment to 'merica. When he got his wish, they were like gold. He ravished them all. The words he read changed his outlook on life.

The sentiment he felt for Malcolm X was akin to adoration. He could not think of Malcolm without reverence. But he was up against his own family and the people in Woodlands who thought the prospect of Jamaicans ruling themselves foolishness. "Marcus Garvey is an ID-IOT!" Someone even told him that "black people can run but should never run anything." Their patriotism to the Queen of England was strong and amounted to idolatry, and whoever spoke against Her Highness incurred the hatred of the entire community. Garnett was often accused of talking rubbish. The process of decolonizing their minds would be long and ordious. In Woodlands, even with the Civil Rights struggle and the USA-Soviet Union Cold War between Communism and Capitalism that lead to the Cuban revolution and the rise of Mr. Fidel Alejandro Castro Ruz to power did not faze them. The people lived in tranquility, far from world politics and its vexations. Family prayers were said in every house the first thing in the morning and the last thing at night. No food was ever partaken without asking God's blessings before AND after the meal.

While Woodlands people were filled with tempestuous emotions and liable to passionate outbursts over irrelevant causes, they mostly cared little about what was going on beyond their solitude and did not appreciate anyone challenging their beliefs and superstitions. Many of them were susceptible to superstitions as these beliefs were handed down generation after generation. Some of them never went to school and those who attended faithfully had teachers who were not equipped to enlighten them.

They were sure that they were right about everything and no one could change their minds. They had two books in their homes, the Sanky (Hymnal) and the Holy Bible, the direct Word of God Almighty, maker of heaven and earth. They took everything they read in the Bible literally and the Queen of England was next to God in their determination of who was important in the universe. Ms. Minnet carried an umbrella to keep off the rain but more importantly, while the sun was shining, to keep her skin from getting darker. She always put on seven layers of clothes each morning as she was told that is how the Queen dressed (panty, pantaloon, slip, chemise, flannel, frock and finally an apron and hat). So while the mercury was leaking out of the top of thermometers and she sweated profusely, she would endure the discomfort as it was more important to be proper than to be comfortable.

Garnett's books inspired and aroused him to become a rebel with a cause and a philosopher in his own mind. He was not afraid of either being laughed at or ridiculed. While he called Malcolm by his first name, he delighted in saying, "Mr. Marcus Mosiah Garvey." Garvey's influence was manifest. Just the mention of the name brought about great reverence. When he was called "a no-good black boy" by haters in the community, infused with self-righteousness, he boastfully quoted Garvey, "This black skin is not a badge of shame. It is a glorious symbol of greatness." Those who heard him spout off what he believed often asked, "Wha im say?" and the answer was invariably "mi no know. Di boy mad." In fact, one gentleman told him, "Boy, I have a feeling that if you wanted to go crazy, it wouldn't be a long journey and if you didn't watch your speed you could overrun yourself." When he took offense, he would say, "And you have trouble counting to two because one gets in your way. You ignoramus!" But mostly, he didn't take offense at these remarks, as by now, he had become indifferent to daily persecutions. Everyone in Woodlands was acquainted with his escapades as he was the topic of repeated conversations.

His mother would ask him to blow out the kerosene lamp with the "Home Sweet Home" written on the glass shade but he was never quite ready for sleep and stayed up reading as long as his stamina would last. Finally, when he fell asleep dreaming of great achievements, he would be rudely awakened when he fell off the chair and hit his head on the floor. When he read books during the day, he sometimes fell asleep dreaming with the book open over his face. When he read, "To have once been a criminal is no disgrace. To remain a criminal is the disgrace" from his hero Malcolm, he promised to never steal again and committed himself to live an honorable life. It left a great impression on him when Malcolm said, "Don't condemn if you see a person drinking a dirty glass of water, just show them the clean glass of water that you have. When they inspect it, you won't have to say that yours is better. You really would have to be insane to drink dirty water when you have access to clean water."

He understood that people would not choose to be criminals or to live in squalor if they had a choice. While everyone he knew thought it was disgusting for Tommi Smith and John Carlos to give the black power salute on the podium of the 1968 Olympic Games, he was motivated by it. He had a lot of fight in him particularly now that he shouted "Black Power" at every opportunity and often held his fist over his head and sang out for everyone to hear, "Say it loud, I am black and I'm proud." While he never backed down from a fight, he never understood why saying good things and feeling good about himself made people upset with him. It puzzled him why black pride was not a virtue and not the sin people made it out to be. He nevertheless resolved to stand up for himself as he felt alone in his newly found pride. It seemed he would use every opportunity to damage himself in the eyes of the community, but as an irascible child, his quick temper made him a formidable adversary, particularly when teacher tried to take away his sacred books.

Three bigger boys ambushed him around Tank way (where the Parish Water Tank is located) to bring him down a peg. They regretted it, as they planned to fight with their fists, and he picked up a "rock stone" and all three of them went home with their heads bloody and bowed. He promised himself to survive by any means necessary. After a while, if there was an "unnatural hurricane" in Woodlands, Garnett was always in the middle of it.

His grandmother asked Minister Hayden Todd to counsel him. When they met, Minister asked him to stop fighting and encouraged him to turn the other cheek, "Do good to your enemies and bless them that hurt or even despise you." Garnett replied, "Sorry, Minister, it's in self-defense. If anybody tries to harm me, I am going to make sure they never do it again." Minister could never win an argument with Garnett, but preached to him about the sanctity of life, honesty being the best policy, and his obligation to his fellow brothers and sisters. Garnett listened but came back with, "Pastor, why should I want to be friends with anybody who don't respect me." Garnett still had the proverbial chip on his shoulder and remained generally contentious.

Among the tactics for revenge he perfected, was learning how to step on a man's corn toe, pinch or "juck" him with the "macka" of his wit and sharp tongue, especially those who scorned him. He knew better than anyone else when someone was lying, and he enjoyed tearing the masks off pretentious people, sometimes leaving them on the defensive by revealing embarrassing secrets that everyone knew but would not dare mention in public. His easy victims were those with unusual sexual practices, those with family secrets as well as those who were too short, bald headed, "maaga" (emaciated looking) or who had pimples and bumps on their face and their head back. He once told a cross eyed man: "Your eyes are so crossed, you could stand in your front yard and count the chickens in the back yard." He was always quick to say exactly what he thought.

Whenever Garnett was confronted by an adversary, he could blow them out like a candle because he always knew their weaknesses. He mostly used well selected words, but he could back it up with his fists and his willingness to confront others regardless of the age difference between himself and his enemies. Sometimes, people he attacked wouldn't know that their legs were cut off until they tried to walk. In addition to his own insecurities, at the core of his beliefs was that he did not believe that rich people were entitled to live in luxury and comfort at the expense of hard working poor people who "sleep on the hard ground with a rock stone for their pillow. When will poor people stop subsidizing rich people? The rich of Jamaica receive a substantial discount on everything, especially people's labor."

As much as the children were advised to avoid Garnett, they would secretly meet to talk with him sitting under a rose apple tree by Benji's pond. He anxiously and deliberately shared what he learned from his books, and his audience kept quiet and listened more intently than they ever did sitting at their desks at school. He confessed to his secret friends that he did not understand how black people could treat their family and friends worse than they treated strangers or even their enemies. What a waste to fight with the people we love! It weighed heavily on his mind, and he was both puzzled and troubled by it. He couldn't explain people's attraction and graciousness to those who abuse them. He didn't think the crumbs they got in return were worth it.

After these discussions, the boys would strip naked, put their clothes under the ginnep tree. Romping and laughing, chasing and splashing each other with the cool water, falling frequently over the bamboo chinas that were submerged in the water as well as slip on the cow dung as the cows looked on curiously. They inevitably got up running again screaming and giggling as they went. Years later, while he was a soldier fighting in a war in Africa, those jejune halcyon days at Benji's pond would become fond memories that brought smiles to his face.

While he was walking behind a teacher and a girl, he overheard the white female teacher tell the student that she should not marry her black boyfriend because she needed cream in her coffee. As Garnett was prone to question his elders, he chimed in without an invitation. "So what you are saying is if your coffee is strong, weaken it by adding milk? The coffee that used to wake you up may now put you to sleep." His audacity infuriated his teacher, and she went to the headmaster to complain about what a troublemaker Garnett had become. She encouraged the Head Master to expel him from school but another teacher spoke up for him and said that she found Garnett to be a very bright boy so he got away with a warning to stop his impudence and foolish talk.

Garnett became more resolute than ever. He felt that he was being lied to at every opportunity. He defied his grandmother when she told him that night air would make him sick. She went so far as to use rags and old newspapers to plug up holes in the walls of their house to keep out the night air. Garnett purposely went out and challenged her professed wisdom and did not become sick.

While he was out walking around one night, he saw a large elderly neighbor enter her outdoor pit toilet and the irresistible thought came to him to turn over the little house. When he did, she became exposed sitting on her throne in the moonlight. This otherwise humble God fearing woman screamed with great horror, threatening to kill the guilty party and in her haste to pull herself together stumbled over her drawers and fell flat on her face with her arms stretched out in front of her spreading the pile of corn cobs. He enjoyed a devilish laugh as he ran off undetected.

To the amazement of his school mates, he delighted in pointing at graves and tombstones without his finger rotting off. He walked home from school in the rain without an umbrella, and people shouted from their houses that he was going to catch his death of cold but he continued to walk home wondering why they didn't all get sick when they took a bath. He was advised that drinking coffee would prevent him from learning his book, but he loved coffee and insisted on having it with his grandmother each morning. He liked it the Zerefa way: plenty of sugar, milk and a pinch of salt.

While he was repeatedly warned that people who sit on the ground would develop a big growth on their shoulder like Gorgie Pokas (a deformed man who lived in the village), he did not see the harm in sitting down wherever he liked. He often heard that cow cod soup is for men only, and if women drank it, it would make their hair fall out. He didn't believe it but could never find a girl willing to take the chance. He did just the opposite when his grandmother told him to get off on the right side of his bed and to put on his right shoes first or he would have bad luck.

The mongoose assumed unusual power because when the mongoose ran across the road, it was good luck but if he turned back after going half way, it was bad luck. Once, his grandmother was taking a hamper of yams to New Market to sell when a mongoose crossed the road ahead of her. But the mongoose changed his mind and went back. Zerefa became alarmed and changed her mind about going to market that day.

Garnett and his brothers organized a posse and jucked sticks in walls until the mongoose tried to escape. They would then run after it and beat it to death with their sticks to evryone's gratitude as chickens were their preferred meal.

The duppy stories that terrified the other "pickney dem" only made Garnett shrug his shoulders and held out his arms showing his "hand middle." But the bravest thing that Garnett ever did was to spend the night in a grave yard to try to find out exactly what goes on at midnight. It got his "curious up" when he was told amazing stories about how duppies (ghosts) came out of their graves at night to hold meetings, sing, dance, roamed the countryside and become Rolling Calves to frighten people. So he tried to recruit some friends to spend a night in a graveyard. "Yu mad?" "Yu wa fi dead?" He answered, "Mi hard man fi dead." His mother was terrified by the idea but knew that when Garnett set his mind to do something nobody could talk him out of it, so she handed him a pillow, a blanket and a flashlight. As it got dark, he went off to spend the night alone in the graveyard up at the church on top of a grave stone and lived to tell about it. It was, however, not a restful night. In the few hours he slept, he was interrupted by every flutter and every noise he heard that made him doubt the wisdom of his decision. The next day, when he returned from the grave, they called him the "Duppy Conqueror," and he was a hero to all who heard about it, but no one else could be persuaded to repeat the experiment.

He actually enjoyed memorizing poems and found them inspirational. The iambic pentameter hypnotized him and took hold of his imagination, so his recitations were highly spirited. With coaching from Ms. Mavis Smith, he won two elocution contests at the St. Elizabeth Cultural Festival in Santa Cruz. In the first year, he recited Claude McKay's poem, "Spanish Needle."

Lovely dainty Spanish needle
With your yellow flower and white,
Dew bedecked and softly sleeping,
Do you think of me to-night?

Shadowed by the spreading mango,
Nodding o'er the rippling stream,
Tell me, dear plant of my childhood,
Do you of the exile dream?

Do you see me by the brook's side?
Catching crayfish 'neath the stone,
As you did the day you whispered,
Leave the harmless dears alone?

Do you see me in the meadow?
Coming from the Woodlands spring
With a bamboo on my shoulder
And a pail slung from a string?

Do you see me all expectant?
Lying in an orange grove,
While the swee-swees sing above me,
Waiting for my elf-eyed love?

Lovely dainty Spanish needle,
Source to me of sweet delight,
In your far-off sunny southland
Do you dream of me to-night?

In the second year, he recited "If" by Rudyard Kipling:

If you can keep your head when all about you

Are losing theirs and blaming it on you;
If you can trust yourself when all men doubt you,
But make allowance for their doubting too:
If you can wait and not be tired by waiting,
Or, being lied about, don't deal in lies,
Or being hated don't give way to hating,
And yet don't look too good, nor talk too wise;

If you can dream—and not make dreams your master;
If you can think—and not make thoughts your aim,
If you can meet with Triumph and Disaster
And treat those two impostors just the same:.
If you can bear to hear the truth you've spoken
Twisted by knaves to make a trap for fools,
Or watch the things you gave your life to, broken,
And stoop and build 'em up with worn-out tools;

If you can make one heap of all your winnings
And risk it on one turn of pitch-and-toss,
And lose, and start again at your beginnings,
And never breathe a word about your loss:
If you can force your heart and nerve and sinew
To serve your turn long after they are gone,
And so hold on when there is nothing in you
Except the Will which says to them, "Hold on!"

If you can talk with crowds and keep your virtue,
Or walk with Kings—nor lose the common touch,
If neither foes nor loving friends can hurt you,
If all men count with you, but none too much:
If you can fill the unforgiving minute
With sixty seconds' worth of distance run,
Yours is the Earth and everything that's in it,
And—which is more—you'll be a Man, my son!

Throughout his life, these two poems became the core of his beliefs and inspiration, which he recited publicly and almost daily to himself.

When Sports Day, the biggest day of the school year arrived, Garnett was ready. The entire community came out to watch the students compete. Mass Claudie McDonald, Mass. Harry Chen See and Mass. Lynn Salmon, the local shop owners contributed the prizes. The vendors sold cakes, sweetie, coconut drops, grater cake, ice cream, cane and cane juice, jellies and aerated water, patties and jerk pork were ever present and created a festive atmosphere. Garnett especially liked the cakes Miss Hibert made. Each "House" (team) actually built a house of bamboo and coconut leaves in an all out effort to outdo the other houses, so no expense or effort was spared on decorating.

The student body was divided into four "Houses." Garnett belonged to Punctuality House and Mrs. Joyce Chang, the wife of the head master, Mr. Clifford Chang, was the teacher/advisor. She was a no-nonsense type of person who made liberal use of the strap. Garnett was elected captain of Punctuality house and was responsible for assigning the competitors for each event.

The other houses were: Politeness, Perseverance and Honesty. The teacher advisers were Mr. Tomlinson, Ms. Nation, and Ms. Mavis Smith, the sweetest, most attentive and most caring teacher Garnett ever had. She was the only teacher who never raised her voice or used the strap and was loved by all. Every student was anxious to make her every wish a command.

In addition to the team sports, each house entered two students for the individual events. Garnett laughed hysterically during volleyball practice when the team members would not stop horsing around. He got upset about it and wanted his team members to become more focused. So he yelled in a strong voice, "stop playing!" So they obliged him by walking off the field.

The sports day events were:

1. Jump rope

2. high jump

3. 100 yards

4. 220 yards

5. 440 years

6. 880 yards

7. potato race

8. egg and spoon race

9. sack race

10. volleyball

11. net ball

12. two legged race

13. Wheelborrow race

14. relays

15. Tug of war

Winners of each event received a gift (pen, wallet, various balls, handkerchief, hat, pen knife and sometimes even money.) Not only did Punctuality House prevail, Garnett was crowned the boys champion with seven presents, his brother Patrick won a belt and a comb while Joshie came home with a cup and saucer.

Garnett was determined to beat his rivals (Devon McDonald, who they called battery, Barryington Stewart, Basil Cameron, Windom Ferqueson, Moses Mckenzie, Gilbert Wright, Tony Row and George Stephenson). Having just learned to recite a poem that included the lines, "While their companions slept were toiling upward in the night," a month before sports day, Garnett marked out a track on his family property with "White wash" and unnoticed by anyone, practiced every morning and evening. He was ready. It probably helped as well that he ran wearing the sneakers Aunt Beryl gave him for Christmas while almost everyone else went barefoot. He won four running events as well as the egg and spoon race as he hard boiled his egg so when he dropped it, he could pick it up and replaced it in his spoon. The last event of the day was the jump rope contest, and he was tied with Devon who won the high jump and some of the running events. Garnett was the only boy who had enough nerve to enter this traditionally girl's event, so he and Carolyn represented Punctuality House, won the event and won the day!

Between his fourteenth and fifteenth birthday, even though several girls were in love with him and even wrote him poems that they slipped into his pockets, he developed a powerful liking for Carolyn Dennis, a pretty girl from the neighboring town of Brighton. She was said to have a good heart, a sweet spirit and a keen sense of justice. The relationship started when he was shaking her hand during the ceremonies on Sports Day, and he tickled her palm and she squeezed his thumb, which signaled to him that she liked him as well. Her spirit just took to him. As the daughter of rigidly puritanical parents, she was expected to be serious about her studies and dress modestly. She didn't even wear a bangle or pierced ear rings like the other girls and yet her face reflected the sweetness and sincerity of her spiritual nature.

When they talked, she wanted to know how him "take lick so" as she thought it was intolerably painful when she took licks in her palms or when her father peppered her ankle with a switch. Garnett was her hero but she made it abundantly clear to him not to try anything as she was not about to do "it" with any boy. He said, "What you take me for? I respect my sisters. I am only trying to keep your company."

He settled on walking her home whenever the opportunity presented itself, especially when he had Boys Brigade meetings where he learned to tie knots with ropes, study the Bible, drill like soldiers, compete in sports and learn survival strategies. She attended "Upward and Onward" after school on Wednesdays at the Moravian Church where she learned cooking and sewing as well as other homemaking skills. They talked often about God and religion. His resistance and protest to religion notwithstanding, she remained steadfast in her faith. He would try to convince her that "God has nothing to do with religion." She would respond, "I love a God that loves and protects me. The more I praise and honor him, the more I am blessed. That's all. For non-believers, heathens and infidels like you, no proof of his existence and His church is ever enough, while the faithful like me don't need proof and don't question." "I don't mean to argue" he said, "but there is no virtue in ignorance. We should all seek truth." "But Garnett, there is no truth. One man's bread is another man's poison. Every time someone, even my teachers tell me something, I find that the opposite can also be true. So to me, truth is whatever each of us believe." He was impressed with her logic and how eloquently she expressed herself. He had underestimated her all along. It was like sunshine after a rain. He found someone he could talk with on a high level. In his excitement, he was like a gushing spring trying to discuss other things he had been thinking about.

On one of these walking and talking occasions, he happened to see an anthill, and once the idea fell into his brain, he couldn't help himself, so he guided Carolyn to sit down and talk with him. In the minute after unwittingly sitting in the ants nest, she started to get stings and cried out in distress, repeatedly saying, "Jesus Christ, Jesus Christ, Jesus Christ." She instantly stripped off all her clothes, and he helped as best he could by slapping the ants from all over her body. He felt a thrill in his groin and soon found himself tormented with desire as something very hard came up between them. But it was no use. Carolyn yelled out, "Yu sadistic brute! Yu too bad!" and pushed him into the pond creating a big splash; shucked the ants from her clothes before putting them back on and running away. While Carolyn ran off, he remained in the cold water until his tempest cooled. He eventually stopped panting like a dog and lost the lead in his pencil with a hearty laugh. He continued to laugh with evil joy as he made his way home.

When Carolyn got home, she reflected on what "that bad boy" did to her and had a good laugh over it herself. In fact, she couldn't help feeling how exciting it was for her, and it came to her on her pillow that they were "doing it" that night. On her way to school the following day, she pulled some "love weed" (68) and yelled out "Garnett Myrie," spit on it and threw it over her shoulder. It landed on some seresee bush that was growing by the side of the road. A week later, the entire bush was glowing with the yellow threads of gold. It made her feel happy and knew she would marry him some day.

Garnett turned fifteen years old and had to leave school as that was as much public education that was provided in Jamaica. As he never had a birthday party or knew how old he was at any particular time, he was surprised when the headmaster came to tell him that he could not return to school. This development was a great relief to the headmaster, several teachers and fellow students who could finally exhale.

As he and Carolyn were the same age, she was also leaving elementary school at the same time but she was hired to assist her mother as a pretrained pupil teacher at St. Elizabeth Technical School for two years. From there, she enrolled in Shortwood Teacher's College between 1973 and 1976, passed the exams to receive a teaching certificate and started teaching at Barking Lodge All Age School in St. Thomas before transferring to Kingston to teach at John Mills Primary.

Garnett was sixteen when his mother decided to migrate to England to be with her husband. She was comfortable leaving her sons, Patrick and Joshie in Woodlands who had already become small farmers working the family land but she wrote a letter to her sister, Beryl Burchel, a dressmaker, who lived in Kingston begging her to take Garnett as he was getting in trouble in Woodlands. His auntie agreed to take him. The following Friday, Mother and son boarded Pinnock's Leyland truck that carried the market women with their vegetables to Kingston to sell in "Curry"(Coronation Market). Garnett was destined to live with his Auntie, while his mother would eventually make her way to Norman Manley Airport for her flight to England.

The truck driver dutifully stopped at Middle Quarters so everyone could get a bag of hot spicy shrimps and then at Spur Tree Hill so everyone could buy their lunch either at "Brownman" or "Blackman" restaurants across the road from each other. So those who identified with the Jamaica Labour Party (JLP) went to "Brownman" and those who were members of the Peoples National Party (PNP) bought their curry goat and rice from "Blackman."

Occasionally, where the hill was particularly steep, the men were asked to get out and walk to reduce the weight. Two helpers would walk with a plank beside the truck to cotch the back wheels every so often to keep the truck from rolling backward and losing ground. The road got much better after Mandeville. The passengers bought oranges in Porus, Manchester, roast cashews in Clarendon, and they could track how far they were from Kingston with growing excitement because the towns were named Nine Mile, Seven Mile, Six Mile down to One Mile.

As they entered the city, music, sweet music was coming from every direction. When the music was not blaring, it was the noise of the trucks, car horns, people cussing and shouting at each other. Toward the end of their journey, seeing the crowd was exciting on the one hand and intimidating on the other. He had never seen so many people, so many cars, so many buildings so close to each other, so many vendors selling everything under the sun. He took particular note of the many members of the Jamaica Constabulary Force dressed smartly in their blue uniforms with the red stripe down each side. Garnett did not take to the rank smell of the city. So he mostly pinched his nose to block out the odor.

His Aunt met them on Oxford Street where all the trucks from St. Elizabeth parked and took them by taxi to her home on

Asquith Street where she assigned him a room. Two days later, they boarded another taxi for the Airport in Port Royal. Enroute, Garnett's aunt pointed out the tall buildings downtown and the mineral bath.

It was not a pleasant good bye. In her last words of advice to him at the airport, his mother criticized Garnett for keeping company with black girls. "Don't bring home anybody whey mi haffi tek light fi look fa. If yu know wha good fi you, you would get friendly with Brownings. Mi only looking out for you." His response to her was, "So you wouldn't approve if I marry someone that looks like you?" She thought it was a facey impertinent comment, so she cut her eye, kissed her teeth and walked away from him without a hug or a kiss to board her BOAC flight to London.

Within a week, his Aunt had secured a job for him as a security guard where one of her friends worked. He loved the job because it provided him with spending money, and he was able to read when he was just sitting around. He learned how to shoot guns and to arrest people as well as see the beautiful homes and luxurious cars he was hired to guard.

The rich of Jamaica separated themselves from everyone else by building their homes in the inaccessible hills around Kingston that only maids, gardeners, and guards would see. In one home where he was assigned to guard, he asked one of the helpers to give him a tour of the place. (Mek mi look the place no?") She agreed and invited him in when the owners were away, but he was timid about it as he was afraid that his very presence would break the dainty and expensive-looking china, glass, and silver. He had never seen such fine furnishings.

The beauty and richness of the fine leather, mahoe furniture and book lined shelves in the room filled him with wonder. He had actually never seen a library before and looked on with envy as he thought to himself how wonderful it would be to read all those books. The statues, medals, and awards, objects of art and quaint and interesting trinkets that must have been brought back from faraway places as well as velvet draperies over the windows introduced him to the life of the rich. He wondered why the inhabitants of these lovely homes seemed so highly favored and surrounded by superior advantages. He perceived that they had limitless plenty. In the homes of the rich, there was never a hint of untidiness, everything was calming to the eye with everything, and everyone was assigned to a special place.

For a country bumpkin growing up without indoor plumbing, he marveled at the furnishing and seven toilets in the house and wondered out loud what the other toilet bowl beside the main toilet (a bidet) was for. He turned the faucet handle and water sprayed his face and wet the floor to the amusement of the maid giving him the tour. He wondered if this is how rich people washed their faces. What impressed him most were not the seven cooks and servants, or the seven bedrooms but the theater that seated fifty people.

There were four domino tables under thatched roofs in the yard where domino tournaments were held every Saturday. Red pea soup, pepper pot and pumpkin beef soup always accompanied dominoes. These rich and powerful movers and shakers came from as far away as Montego Bay, Hanover, Portland and Ocho Rios to participate in Saturday Soup that was served by an all black staff. The house had a parking lot that accommodated twenty cars, mostly Jaguars and Mercedes Benz. While men played dominoes, smoked cigars, and drank beer and rum punch, the children played hop scotch, jumped rope or danced and the well-dressed ladies sipped on sour sop juice and gossiped by the swimming pool. They giggled and laughed while the black chauffeurs, gardeners, yard boys and butlers held their summit under the mango tree when they were not otherwise doing their master's will.

Garnett was awed by the view. Toward dusk and as the evening shadows moved across the sky, the bougainvillea-shrouded walls of the compound took on a beautiful yellow haze. Garnett could see the glowing arch of a complete rainbow that stretched from east to west with Kingston Harbour reflecting the emerging sunset on the tall buildings in the background. Behind him were the Blue Mountains dotted with brilliant red flowers and cloud puffs hanging over them like cotton balls. He commented to his guide, "What a way white people live good man!"

But on the other side of town was a violent brutish place where he expected to be cheated at every turn. Under their bludgeoning circumstances, no one can do right and live. What is right conduct under these circumstances? Who is willing to sacrifice themselves for principles or compassion for those less fortunate? The old, the young, those compromised with illness become easy victims. Mothers scream one command after another at barefoot children in their desperate attempt to protect their progeny.

The resourcefulness of the poor making homes on captured lands out of cardboard, burned out cars, pieces of discarded zinc and slabs of wood was widespread. Raw sewage and the stench of decay run down gullies. These are villages of desperation where women and children live with unspeakable sorrow.

Their ambitions for a better life died as they gradually recognize that there were no viable jobs for which they could sensibly aspire. Violence with guns, knives, machetes, rock stones and whatever could be fashioned into a weapon was in common use. Garnett found Kingston ghettos to be wild and untamable where lionhearted boys do what they do, getting killed or maimed with no fear of death. People who live in this environment were all sweetness with each other until they disagreed. They had no ability to amicably resolve their disputes except with abusive contentious arguments that often ended with someone being killed. Fighting and killing each other was frequent. They just did not know how to live without violence. For those who grew up in this environment, it was all normal but it was alien to Myrie, the country boy—even one used to bullying others.

On his way home from his job one evening, he passed four Kingston Ginals with menacing countenances that made him apprehensive. He tried to be friendly and greeted them, but one of them asked him if he had ever heard of the "Vikings." When he responded that he didn't, they said he was about to become acquainted. They shouted obscenities and attacked him, stole his money as well as the watch his father sent him from England two Christmas's ago, smashed his right foot with a big stick and almost put out his left eye with their fists. They mercifully did not kill him. He tried to get a ride home but no one stopped. He was crawling through a rich neighborhood, and when he could go on no more, he cried out louder and louder for help. No one came to his rescue but eventually someone from a nearby house called the police complaining that someone was making a disturbance. The police unsympathetically and suspiciously took him to his aunt's house, and eventually, Aunt Beryl brought him by taxi to Kingston Public Hospital where they fixed his broken foot and bandaged his face and eye after a six hour wait.

In his conversation with his aunt while he was recuperating, she asked him what he had learned about life so far in Kingston. In a response that surprised her, he said he had learned that black people seem to have no rights that rich people respect, and that they had no needs that those in power were inclined to address. Everything favor the wealthy and penalize the poor. Jamaican black people are brutally oppressed. It's as if white people are at war with us. If a White man hit a black man in the face, he believed the black man would be charged with using his face to hit the white man's fist. (When he repeated this claim to Dr. Walter Rodney sometime later, he was told that a nobleman in England, Edward de Vere, a contemporary of William Shakespeare, had in fact, murdered a household servant in anger and the judge found him not guilty as the servant must have ran into his sword. "Nobody befriends us and just about everybody joins in hating, abusing and persecuting black people, and we take it. We are our own worst enemy. How did we come to respect and love everybody else more than our own family and friends?"

CHAPTER II

Mr. Myrie's Adventures

With his black affirming proclivities, he marveled at the shackles of English legacy that prevented black people from sharing his perspective. But he kept trying. In formulating their internal belief system, he was frustrated that Jamaican people had no inclination to test what they were told. So what they believed came down from slave masters, English ministers, and brainwashed teachers. This was the source of much of their unchallenged knowledge to make the colonial version of reality more believable than their own powers of observation. Instead of falling victims to this collective delusion, he believed they needed a new form of common sense that he believed he alone possessed. They all knew that there was no difference between white horses and black horses, black cats and white cats, but when it came to people, white people were superior (except as dance and sex partners, physical labor, tolerating the sun's harsh rays and athletic performance). Garnett went to great lengths and took advantage of every opportunity to offer a new way at looking at their lives and their beliefs, but he came upon great resistance. The alarm he raised did not register with his audience.

Feeling particularly frustrated with how difficult it was to persuade acquantances to his righteous cause, he read in the Gleaner that Dr. Martin Luther King, the icon of the civil rights movement in the United States was scheduled to speak at the University of the West Indies on June 20, 1965. The article explained that it was controversial to have him speak in Jamaica as many in power feared what he may stir up in Jamaica. Professor Anthony Allen thought he would be an inspiration to the poor prevailed and arranged for the great civil rights leader to address a Jamaican audience. It turned out to be an important occasion for both Rev. King and his Jamaican hosts. Dr. King readily admitted that: "In Jamaica, I feel like a human being." His message to the 400 people who attended was:

"No work is insignificant. All labor that uplifts humanity has dignity and importance and should be undertaken with painstaking excellence . . . Everybody can be great . . . because anybody can serve. You don't have to have a college degree to serve. You don't have to make your subject and verb agree to serve. You only need a heart full of grace. A soul generated by love . . . If a man is called to be a street sweeper, he should sweep streets even as a Michaelangelo painted, or Beethoven composed music or Shakespeare wrote poetry. He should sweep streets so well that all the hosts of heaven and earth will pause to say, 'Here lived a great street sweeper who did his job well."

Garnett had never met a man with so much charisma. His eloquence and wit was inspiring. He left the campus of the University of the West Indies inspired. While he had read about Dr. King, meeting him in person was life changing.

After many hours of debating the injustice of Jamaican society with his coworkers, one of the other security guards took him to hear a speech by Dr. Walter Rodney, a renowned but controversial history professor at the University of the West Indies. Having been born March 23, 1942, in Guyana, Dr.

Rodney had come of age as a scholar and political activist at twenty-five years old. He was nine years older than Garnett.

While the Prime Minister Hugh Shearer insisted that Jamaica's mother country was England. "This is the source of our laws, our language, government, literature, and education. Why would anyone, especially educated ones, choose to identify with the Butu people of Africa? What did we get from Africa?"

Dr. Rodney preached that black man time had come. All who heard his lectures affectionately referred to him as the African Doctor. Prime Minister Shearer respected Dr. Rodney's scholarship but considered him an agitator and troublemaker. Dr. Rodney certainly looked the part with an Afro hairstyle, a beard, wearing a multicolored dashiki and horrors of horrors he professed his admiration for the Black Panthers, Chi Guevara, Castro, and the other Black Power advocates in the United States. He even told his university students that if they really wanted to learn and raise their conscientiousness, they should sit by the knees of their Rasta Bretherin who everyone else considered illiterate unwashed fools. While Rodney was a professor at the University of the West Indies, he was conveniently not a Jamaican by birth.

After Garnett heard one of Dr. Rodney's speeches, it was like listening to himself. "De man knows what him a say. It's pure truth him a preach." Garnett was impressed that this black man studied in England and was a respected professor who wrote books. He introduced himself to Dr. Rodney and the two of them hit it off immediately. They spent the entire first night debating and discussing everything that was on his mind and never felt either hungry, sleepy, or even tired. His reverence for Dr. Rodney was deep and genuine and he prized the newfound friendship. He kept saying to Dr. Rodney, "You right, you right, you right." With so many cathartic moments during the night, he felt like a new man who had been transformed and reborn with a clear understanding of the society in which he lived. The last thing Dr. Rodney said to him before departing was: "Nam et ipsa scientia potestas est". Knowledge is power.

Garnett was also impressed with Robin "Bongo Jerry" Small, who was a graduate of Jamaica College and was brought up as a privileged member of the Middle Class but who had joined the Brethren and operated as the go between for Dr. Rodney and the Rastafarians. Bongo Jerry introduced Dr. Rodney as a man for all seasons that could, "inform the head and melt the heart."

In one of their somber moments, Garnett asked, "Professor, it makes me sick that so many a wi tief so much and drown each other in this sea of violence? Are Jamaicans just mad? Why we are always trying to take other people's property and killing each other? Why would a thief let an honest man plow up him ground, plant his crop, weed and care for it and then steal his cow and crop before the rightful owner can benefit from the sweat of his brow?"

Brother Wally got into his professorial mode and explained, "You have probably never heard of a Austrian psychiatrist by the name of Sigmund Freud but I believe he had a lot to say about the personalities in Jamaica.

I often ask friends who they believe are the most powerful people in Jamaica. Are they gunmen? Dons? Politicians? Religious leaders? Rich people? Policemen or babies? If you define power as one's ability to quickly get what they want, then the answer is a crying child. The distressed child, who is hungry, wants his diaper changed or who wants comfort will cry until his needs are met. Nature programmed us to respond urgently to children's crying.

A child is all "Id." A child has no ability to delay gratification or consider anyone else's needs, "I want what I want when I want it." "If I itch, I want it scratched." Some of us never grow out of this immaturity. "I will kill anybody who disrespects me." These are the bad minded people who always want something for nothing and who want to prosper at someone else's expense. This childish conduct can be quickly recognized on the roads from the drivers who put everyone at risk by inappropriately overtaking others because only their needs matter. The other day I witnessed an accident because one of the speeding taxies decided it needed to drive on the wrong side of the road and incorrectly merge into traffic only to run into the car that had the right of way. Everyone at this point was inconvenienced; the passengers of the bus, the cars behind the accident and the driver whose car was smashed.

Ordinarily, as one matures, we learn a reality principle or the cause and effect rules of life which Freud calls the "ego." If I put my hand in a fire, it will burn. If I fall down, it will hurt. If I steal or otherwise break the law, the police will arrest and imprison me. A healthy fear of punishment takes hold. We learn to value the rights of others and respect boundaries. If I treat others special, they will be kind and helpful to me in my hour of need. If I work hard, develop meaningful skills, knowledge and attitudes, I can find employment or own a business so I can support myself and take care of my family. If there is no family structure or if the rules of society are not predictably enforced, some people will not believe they will be punished for crime and that they can get rich quick and always get their way by intimidating others—including their parents and the police. Killers now believe that they can get away with murder as only a small number of murders are ever solved. Do we really want the world to believe that our country is run by "outlaws"?

Finally, Freud believed that we also develop a superego or a conscience. Our family, our community, our schools, our religious institutions and our culture impress ethics on us. If society is successful, we feel guilty when we don't do "the right thing." We don't want to be disgraced. We are embarrassed if we violate a social code like going to a funeral wearing a bathing suit. Our conscience becomes our guide. If we have a conscience, we are motivated to be kind and generous to needy relatives, the sick and the elderly. If you don't have a conscience, a criminal may even consider robbing the most vulnerable if they have something he or she wants. Let your conscience be your guide.

Ideally, we need a balance. We need the "Id" so we can have a good time. Sex, dancing, partying, playing games, competing, playing tricks on others, telling jokes, laughing and that whoopee feeling all come from the "Id." There is nothing wrong with fun, especially after the work is done, and you have actually accomplished something. We also need to know what is real (ego strength), as well as being responsible parents to restrain the less irresponsible among us from overindulgence and to guide and nurture the next generation. I don't believe we ever want to be so guilt stricken that we need to beat up ourselves every time we have a good time. However, we should also learn that moderation and balance are the keys to a truly successful life.

Imagine a little jockey (our developed ego and superego) riding a big, powerful horse (our Id). Even though the horse weighs ten times more than the jockey, the horse can be skillfully controlled by the jockey. If the horse is unbridled, however, the Id cannot be controlled, and we become undisciplined, unproductive, immoral, and completely selfish.

As a society, if we truly want to stop homicides and theft, we can start with enforcing the rule of law for small infractions, which will lead to stopping the major ones. Jamaica needs solid and unwavering enforcement of the law, first by each individual doing the right thing and in those cases in which a segment of our society refuses to do the right thing; the police can rein them in. As you can see, it becomes a huge problem when the police and the people who work in our legal system become the outlaws.

It is going to take the church, schools, families and all the institutions of society to train the jockey—to develop our ego and superego so that law and order can prevail. I am in a constant debate with my wife, Patricia, about whether God blesses honest, disciplined, hard working considerate people. I believe that good people also succeed because everyone wants to do business with them and crave their company. Who wants to be friends with or do business with people who lie, cheat and commit crimes? Not even criminals like the company of other criminals.

In the final analysis, good people will always prosper because no one ever secures happiness by committing crimes." Garnett responded, "I see what you mean."

Dr. Rodney was a regular at Nyabinghi open yard sessions at the home of Brother Mortimo Planno. They all joined in the drumming, chanting, reasoning, and praise singing to Selassie and Marcus Garvey. This was heightened on 21 April 1966 when Emperor Haile Selassie I of Ethiopia visited Jamaica. As a Head of State, he was honored at King's House by all the noble men and women of Jamaica including (for the first and maybe the last time) Rastafarians.

While Garnett also frequented Bongo Jerry Small's "Open Yard" drumming, licking the chalice (69) and discussing their condition, he was mostly drawn to Dr. Rodney who was also impressed with the youth and invited him to join a group of thinkers at his "groundings."(70) The group included from time to time Dr. Rodney's wife (Patricia), Norman Gavin, Ralph Gonsalves (became Prime Minster of St. Vincent and Granadines), Sam Clayton, Count Ossie (Mystic Revelations of Rastafarians), Ras Dizzy (artist), Pa Ashanti, Rupert Ahwee, Carolyn Cooper, Carol Yawney, Rev. Claudius Henry, Dennis Chin, Robert Hill, Donald (DK) Duncan (Trusted ally to PM Michael Manley and the author of Democratic Socialism),

Leonard Howell, Peter Tosh, Gladstone Edman, Bob Marley, Toddy Livingston, and Tito.

There was great consternation in the group when Reverend Henry's son was executed for murder and treason. It was also a time when black people and Locksmen (Rastafarians) were denied access to jobs, hotels, public parks, and even public beaches. There were heated and prolonged discussions on race relations and the injustice of Jamaican society between the "Groundings" lead by Dr. Rodney and the "Open Yard Reasoning" sessions with drums and "chillum pipes" organized by Mortimo St. George Planno (Brother Kumi) on Fifth Street in Trench Town. This was a turbulent but fertile period of introspection and radical thought for Jamaican intellectuals and musicians. On the other hand, with encouragement from the political leaders, the police were brutal and tried to put them under "heavy manners." (71) Dr. Rodney wailed and railed against the injustices of the colonial minded society. Garnett's frustration over this oppressive police action reminded him of the time he was held down by the hog butchers in Woodlands.

In one of his many street speeches, Dr. Rodney said: "We have petitioned, we have remonstrated, we have supplicated, we have prostrated ourselves, and all it has done is to invite the aggression of our oppressors. While we have an abiding reverence for human life, we have no other option now but to fight. I have learned from history that killing people is the only effective means of securing political freedom and justice because power never yields without a struggle. Those in power doesn't hesitate to kill to retain power but there will never be a shortage of heroes who are willing to give their lives in the cause of freedom. Of course, there will be misery and suffering. Those who own everything in Jamaica have no understanding or sympathy with those who have nothing. We must never accept this brutish and unjust life as normal. We must never accept oppression. The fire that is born with us cannot be quenched. The machete will not sleep in my hands, and my gun will not be silent. We must bring Babylon to its knees. Otherwise, we will never have justice in Jamaica."

Rodney's eloquence could touch the hearts of statues. Garnett thought he possessed a profound understanding for the frailties of mankind and knew the way forward for the Caribbean but those in power would not heed his counsel. Dr. Rodney advised the group that the antidotes offered by our politicians were poison in disguise for the people at large. According to Dr. Rodney: "It is perverse for us to be celebrating three hundred years of enemy occupation. One day, country people will reach the limit of their endurance, wake up and discover that they are entitled to full citizenship and not just beasts of burden working in the dirt to produce cheap food for the privileged. When they do, there will be hell to pay." Garnett was in the audience applauding loudly and yelling, "Black man time now."

Garnett could not get the image out of his mind of Jesus as a child sitting down and debating with the scholars of his day and taking care of his father's business. Like Jesus, Garnett was regularly in the company of grown men in Dr. Rodney's discussion circles. Even at seventeen years old, Garnett became one of Dr. Rodney's disciples. While Dr. Rodney was the "Maximum Leader," they all respected and loved Garnett for his enthusiasm and understanding. Garnett prided himself on being self-made and self-educated and was now ready to put everything aside to dedicate his life to the cause of uplifting the people. He found his calling.

While other youths were all talk and no juice, even without a formal education, Garnett was well read, could talk, quote poetry, give spontaneous speeches, and they all wanted to learn from him as well. Dr. Rodney treated him like an equal, and their relationship blossomed as Garnett's appetite for knowledge increased and Dr. Rodney provided the books and became his Socrates. The end of one of these discussions, Peter Tosh, his comrade, asked Dr. Rodney: "Do you mean that all black people came from Africa?" Dr. Rodney replied: "absolutely. In addition, African was home to the Garden of Eden. All human beings came out of Africa." All the heads in the group went up and down like chickens eating corn.

They often talked about Nelson Mandela and apartheid in South Africa, Malcolm X and Martin Luther King in America, Kwame Nkrumah, Fidel Castro and Chi Guevera, Julius Nyerere, W. E. B. Du Bois, CLR James, and Gandhi. Garnett was particularly impressed with the company he was keeping and carried around a copy of "Groundings with My Brothers", written by Dr. Rodney that he referred to as his bible. He thought Dr. Rodney was a genius at attracting thinking people like milk to a baby. And everyone felt fed listening to him.

Garnett, however, missed the reassuring rhythms of the country. He had come to know bitterness, despair and even hatred. In Kingston, people either learned to steal or starve, fight or run. Garnett quickly acquired cunning and ruthlessness learning that oppression has the effect of turning its victims against each other and playing to their oppressors for favors.

When Dr. Rodney asked Garnett to accompany him in a meeting with the leaders of the "Viking" gang, Garnett thought it was a bad idea but followed the Maximum Leader's directives. Dr. Rodney was trying to forge a strategy to bring all the disaffected groups in Jamaica together. Rev. Alexander Bedword, some Rastafarians, university students and the Viking Gang were the groups he wanted under his umbrella. While Rev. Bedword was on board and gave Dr. Rodney access to his congregations, Dr. Rodney was less influential with the Rastas even though they too affectionately called him "Brother Wally." He wanted the Vikings because the politicians and police feared them and would think twice about attacking his group if he came under the protection of the Vikings. But Garnett wondered who would protect Dr. Rodney from these hoodlums.

Their conference room was under a breadfruit tree with everyone sitting on old tires, blocks of wood and rock stones. Up walked several members of the Viking Gang. Garnett recognized them as the four men who robbed him. One of them was wearing his watch. This angered Garnett and throughout the meeting, he kept quiet and focused on how he was going to get his watch back.

When it got dark and the meeting broke up, Garnett followed the gang. He saw them rob an innocent man at gunpoint as well as lick down the victim with a fist to the victim's face. When each went their own way, Garnett continued to follow the man who was wearing his watch. Just as the Viking Robberman turned a corner, Garnett ran up and hit him over the head with a tire iron he had picked up in the yard, grabbed the watch along with the man's gun, wallet and money and ran off fearing some calamity but got away. As he never saw the gentleman again, he had no idea what became of him. He never inquired and the Viking gang never again participated in Dr. Rodney's plans. Instead, Dr. Rodney turned to the Spangler Gang that operated out of Wildman Street.

Dr. Rodney had a knack for winning over people from all walks of life. He never met a stranger. Soon after meeting someone, they would become comfortable and chatty, but mostly they listened to a genius with answers to Jamaica's problems. He seemed to know everything and forget nothing. He was particularly good at remembering the names of people he met. Garnett admired him for not only being a deep thinker who told them a great deal they did not know but also remaining respectful and considerate of others who were less read. Dr. Rodney wondered out loud what terrible crime the poor people of Jamaica committed to be sentenced to a life of unimaginable deprivations. Their only crime was getting themselves born in the wrong part of town where disease, crime and illiteracy reigned.

Everyone was enriched by being in Dr. Rodney's presence and was soon regarding him as a friend. In addition, he arranged for a free university with evening classes that he called "Piper's Cabin." He even invited colleagues from the University of the West Indies to lecture community people on a wide range of subjects. His attempt to uplift the people through knowledge failed, however, because of harassment from the police. The community was very engaged and excited by what they learned and Garnett in particular never missed the classes. But the Station Chief of the Denham Town Police Station, Mr. Joe Williams, who everyone called "Massa Joe" believed these gatherings were just fermenting revolution and not only found every opportunity to confront both the teachers and the students but also ordered these evening classes closed. Whenever anyone resisted the system, they were met with violence and oppression.

Out of frustration and in protest, Dr. Rodney called another street meeting. In a very animated and passionate speech, Dr. Rodney said it was infuriating that the Caribbean has become a spectacle groveling in contentment refusing to recognize our greatness. He was riling against the prime minister who he referred to as "the Dishonorable Hugh Shearer" and the political elite are just a small group of terrorists who control everything and are a blight on the country because they blatantly and heartlessly ignore the suffering of poor people who continue to live only because it is a habit they cannot break. Every year, banks in imperialistic countries loan countries in the Caribbean huge sums of money that mostly go into the pockets of politicians. But this debt will have to be paid by future generations. When it cannot be paid, our politicians continue to borrow more and put the future of the Caribbean in a straightjacket. How will we ever get these banks off our backs?"

As Dr. Rodney was getting the crowd excited about the plight of the oppressed and their many grievances, Garnett got carried away and shouted, "We have the manpower, you have the brains; all we need are guns." Dr. Rodney responded, "Revolution must come. We must be prepared at some point in time to see it through. Petition, persuasion and the ballot box will never bring about the change we want. We must stop talking and indulging in academic exercises and act. Who will be the first to come with me downtown and take up a gun?' Garnett held up the gun he took from the Viking Gang and shouted back, "I am!" Several others joined in "Yea Mon!" The crowd was finally persuaded to act when Dr. Rodney reminded them that "No English King ever yielded any stolen and unjust right unless it was wrenched from them through violence. Nothing short of bloodshed will bring reform to Jamaica."

When word of Dr. Rodney's rhetoric got back to Prime Minister Hugh Shearer, he not only reasserted that West Indians were not Africans but also declared war on the street movement. The military and police were ordered to clamp down on all protests. He expelled some black Americans who were in Jamaica organizing and spouting "Black Power" and arrested several followers. "Black Power" books were banned, Hugh Masekela, Miriam Makeba and Stokely Carmichael (friends of Dr. Rodney from their days in Guinea Conakry under the Patronage of Prime Minister Ahmed Sekou Toure) were denied permission to visit Jamaica and while attending a conference in Toronto, Dr. Rodney was declared "persona non grata" by the prime minister who Dr. Rodney characterized as the "White Hearted Prime Minister" on October 14, 1968. Dr. Rodney was then forced to return to Canada where his flight originated. Later, Dr. Rodney would take up residence in Cuba under the patronage of Fidel Castro who greatly admired his scholarship.

In response to the news of Dr. Rodney's eviction from Jamaica, riots broke out and Garnett was one of the chief organizers. Their rallying cry was that the prime minister was trying to deny their blackness and their connection to Africa. University students tried to make it a peaceful demonstration walking around in red robes and placards, but Garnett and friends took the initiative to set buildings and cars on fire, yelling, "Fire bun. Idiot ting dis." (72) Three of the people who participated in the riot were killed by the police.

When the police accosted them, Peter Tosh and about a dozen of them took refuge in a firehouse. The police then shot tear gas into the firehouse setting off a firefight between the police and the firemen. Garnett laughed at the spectacle. Peter Tosh then Commandered a city bus, ran it into a department store so everyone could help themselves and then transported them in the same bus to BackAwall. Peter was eventually caught and brutalized by the police and Garnett became a wanted man, could not return to his job and the police searched high and low for him without success as he was hiding and receiving underground support from Cubans. After Prime Minister Shearer lost his seat, Mr. Edward Seaga became the prime minster as head of the Jamaica Labour Party. The new prime minister ordered bulldozers to violently destroy the homes of Rastafarians who were living on a captured piece of land. BackAwall was then developed as a Tivoli Gardens to accommodate his JLP supporters and those displaced moved to Waurika Hills.

Garnett then secretly left for Cuba at Dr. Rodney's invitation in 1970. While in Cuba, Dr. Rodney persuaded him to join the Cuban Army who trained, equipped and sent him to fight in a successful guerrilla campaign in Angola where his life was in jeopardy from every direction.

Garnett returned to Jamaica in 1975, four years after leaving in 1971. Before he left Cuba, he met personally with Fidel Castro, who thanked him for helping to free the people of Angola who were now richer in self-esteem and self-determination than when he went.

On his discharge in 1976 at the ripe old age of twenty-three, he was given a lump sum of American dollars. During his sojourn, the Cubans had also taught him carpentry, construction and architecture. He returned as stealthfully as he left but was now richer, wiser and more confident. He was away for five years and no one had inquired about his whereabouts or whether he was alive or dead. There were no stories or pictures on the front page of the Gleaner, no marching band, no banners fluttering in the wind, no speeches by politicians and religious leaders, expressing the sentiments of a grateful nation for risking his life to free the people of Angola.

On his return, he was to learn that his old friend Peter Tosh was now an international reggae singing sensation riding high with rebellion songs: "Equal Rights", "Get up and stand up", "Legalise it (ganga)"; "If you are a Black man, you are an African", "Steppin' Razor", "Bush Doctor", "Johnny be Good" and "I'm the Toughest". At the "One Love Peace" on April 12, 1978, following Jacob Miller to the stage, Peter was to pay a heavy price for pulling out all stops as he riled against the "shit-stem" that was brutalizing poor people. Some time later, he was accosted by several members of the Jamaican police, severely beaten and imprisoned for his outspokenness. It appeared to Garnett that Peter was keeping Walter Rodney's passions alive as he lashed out at the colonial mentality in Jamaica; he was a guerrilla fighter in Africa and Peter the guerrilla fighter in music—the "Reggae Che Guevera". Garnett was impressed that with all the brutality he had to endure, him no ease up.

Bob Marley left the Island in 1976 for England and was not heard from for two years when he exploded on the scene with "Exodus" that made him a household name throughout the world. "One Love" and "People Get Ready" became Garnett's new mantra that he repeated in almost every conversation. Bob Marley was the last performer at the "One Love Peace Concert" when Michael Manley, leader of the then-ruling People's National Party, who Garnett loved and the leader of the Jamaica Labour Party, Edward Seaga, whose policies he opposed were both present. With the encouragement of Bob Marley, the two leaders shook hands at the end of his sold out performance. Both leaders made a commitment to end Garrison politics and to run a clean election.

Because of Garnett's involvement in the liberation of Angola, the song Bob Marley performed at Zimbabwe's Independence Celebration in 1980 was like a gift from God.

Every man gotta right to decide his own destiny,
And in this judgment there is no partiality.
So arm in arms, with arms, we'll fight this little struggle,
'Cause that's the only way we can overcome our little trouble.

Brother, you're right, you're right,
You're right, you're right, you're so right!
We gon' fight (we gon' fight), we'll have to fight (we gon' fight),
We gonna fight (we gon' fight), fight for our rights!

Natty Dread it in-a (Zimbabwe);
Set it up in (Zimbabwe);
Mash it up-a in-a Zimbabwe (Zimbabwe);
Africans a-liberate (Zimbabwe), yeah.

No more internal power struggle;
We come together to overcome the little trouble.
Soon we'll find out who is the real revolutionary,
'Cause I don't want my people to be contrary.

And, brother, you're right, you're right,
You're right, you're right, you're so right!
We'll 'ave to fight (we gon' fight), we gonna fight (we gon' fight)
We'll 'ave to fight (we gon' fight), fighting for our rights!

Mash it up in-a (Zimbabwe);
Natty trash it in-a (Zimbabwe);
Africans a-liberate Zimbabwe (Zimbabwe);
I'n'I a-liberate Zimbabwe.

(Brother, you're right,) you're right,
You're right, you're right, you're so right!
We gon' fight (we gon' fight), we'll 'ave to fight (we gon' fight),
We gonna fight (we gon' fight), fighting for our rights!

To divide and rule could only tear us apart;
In everyman chest, mm—there beats a heart.
So soon we'll find out who is the real revolutionaries;
And I don't want my people to be tricked by mercenaries.

Brother, you're right, you're right,
You're right, you're right, you're so right!
We'll 'ave to fight (we gon' fight), we gonna fight (we gon' fight),
We'll 'ave to fight (we gon' fight), fighting for our rights!

Natty trash it in-a Zimbabwe (Zimbabwe);
Mash it up in-a Zimbabwe (Zimbabwe);
Set it up in-a Zimbabwe (Zimbabwe);
Africans a-liberate Zimbabwe (Zimbabwe);
Africans a-liberate Zimbabwe (Zimbabwe);
Natty dub it in-a Zimbabwe (Zimbabwe).

Set it up in-a Zimbabwe (Zimbabwe);
Africans a-liberate Zimbabwe (Zimbabwe);
Every man got a right to decide his own destiny

Each time he heard the song, he would say, "It sweet me, it sweet me, it sweet me, it sweet me. Mi proud yu si and pity any man who is not a Jamaican." More importantly, Bob Marley and the Wailers had become the most beloved musicians in all the world. They could count on sold out audiences in literally every venue. The Rasta lifestyle was very much in style as people in Europe, the United States and Japan grew their hair and those who couldn't wore Rasta wigs. Jamaican musicians with dreadlocks were in great demand and brought plenty of foreign exchange to the island. The previously scorned Rastaman became respected and his lifestyle was now enamored by the masses. The ital diet became popular as well and plenty of "rude boys" wanted to become like their new idols—Bob Marley, Peter Tosh and Bunny Wailer.

Garnett was staying at the home of his Aunt Beryl before deciding on his next move. He often thought of Carolyn over the years and was hungry to see her. He learned that she was sick with the Dengue fever and was being cared for by her parents in Brighton. Once a member of the household caught the fever, it quickly spread to everyone else and the entire family felt poorly. Feeling invincible and being fearless of neither man or germ, Garnett bought both his driver's license and an SUV with some of the money he had brought back from Cuba. He made his way to St. Elizabeth battling the bad roads and set about nursing Carolyn with affectionate devotion. His presence was the medicine the family needed as she quickly recovered along with the rest of her family. He was like a breath of fresh air that blew in to cool their fevers.

He slept at his parent's old house in Woodlands and marveled at how much it had shrunk. He could not believe that it had comfortably accommodated over six people when he was a child and how claustrophobic he now felt in it as a man. He went daily to hold Carolyn's hand, wipe her fevered brow with a damp cloth and tell her stories about the Angolan war from which he recently returned. No one in Jamaica knew that he had volunteered to be a guerilla fighter in Africa.

Word got around that Garnett, the impetuous young soldier, was back from war. During his long absence, the good citizens of Woodlands had been guessing as to whether he was in prison or worse. They gathered with eager ears and drank up the liquor he bought as well as listened to his every word hungrily. When Garnett left at sixteen years old, they thought he would become a drug dealer and criminal. When he returned at twenty-four, apparently flush with cash, they now thought him an angel in disguise with the expectation that he would rescue them from their misery with his promises of work. They hoped and prayed nightly for someone to come along and blow the breath of life into a village that was languishing. Garnett, ever faithful to where his navel string was buried, felt at home in Woodlands than anywhere else he had ever been. When he was around, no one else went into their pockets as Garnett paid for everything.

Among the stories they recounted about him was the confession from Alva Billings that he saw Garnett when he was stealing June plums from Mass Clinton's tree and the dog came after him. Alva said he saw Garnett hit the dog with a rock stone and broke the dog's leg. Alva got an extra beer as well as bun and cheese for not divulging his secret until now. Hiram Woodstock reminded Garnett about the day when he confessed that the two of them were looking up through the cracks of the school flooring to see girl's panties for which they got six licks a piece with a strap. "Yea, you got us both in trouble but it was worth it."

Each subsequent evening at the rum shop, in addition to buying beer and rum for everyone, they wanted him to cuss as some of the men said they would rather hear him cuss than to hear another man pray. They even recommended that he do it on stage. "People would pay money to hear you cuss bad word!" Little Man then chirped in, "I never enjoyed profanity more than when you cuss. You are a true artist. Your cussing was like a volcano spewing thunder and lightning. It was something to hear and fear."

When the hour got late and they bid good night each night, they were drunk with happiness. The hopeless was daring to hope again. He was now their darling, and he wanted to meet their every expectation. It appeared that people were sitting on their heels and making no plans beyond the next plate of food, hoping for a "savior" to fix things and make life better, Garnett now assumed this role.

He promised himself that he would not make people dependent on him but would hire people and buy goods and services that he needed. An extinguishing blight fell upon that dream as the sight of the perishing faces (young and old) pierced his generous heart, and he found it discomforting. The young grew up, the old became feeble and melancholy replaced happiness. He could not stand the extreme poverty in which they lived with their outdoor kitchens and latrines—if they were lucky. Some answered the call of nature behind whatever tree was available and used leaves to clean themselves. He could endure life in the jungles of Angola and any amount of beatings and torture that was administered to his body, but his conscience could not stand up to the deplorable living conditions, which he was forced to witness. So he bought a salve for it with a compromise and was generous with his handouts as otherwise he would not be able to sleep. Wherever he went, the palms went out and his hand went into his pocket to pull out wads of cash.

For someone who had spurned the church, he was invited to address the entire congregation who were jubilant in their praise. His return made the entire village glad. Wherever he went people shared their childhood stories of him and complimented him with, "What a way yu turn out good? Yu even drive SUV and dress so nice!"

In his presentation to the congregation, with ringing pride in his voice, he expressed gratitude for indulging him with their attention, described his plans to start various enterprises and finished his presentation with an ode to Woodlands District:

Here where the sun shines
And cool breeze whines
Through mango trees and weeping willows
Sweet dreams on soft feather pillows
Friends big up each other with "respect," "mawnin," and "irie"
Memories to fill a lifetime diary

Stains on my shirt from star apple and jack fruit
Custard apple, carrot juice and beer from ginger root
Jankonoo, duppy stories and nine night wakes
Breadfruit, bammy and black wedding cakes
Baptism before the cricket match at New Pon
My father playing the guitar with the rhumba band, ya mon!

Here is my boyhood home
Unhampered space and gullies to roam
Gifted me pride and an ounce of courage
A taste for run punch, sorrel and cornmeal porridge
Curry goat, escovitched fish, rice and peas, ackee and cod
Woodlands District, Jamaica, gave me my God!

But the thing that looked easy and achievable would prove to be surprisingly difficult. His idea to start up several businesses did not take root and grow. Using local labor, he built the largest house in the district, put up a great wall along the road, taught construction, plumbing and electrical skills to people who were unskilled and set up a carpenter shop fully equipped with saws, clams, polishers, and lathes. He also employed twenty men.

The trouble was that while the community was overwhelmingly supportive, a small group of selfish criminal minded men who suspected the gravy train would not last sabotaged Garnett's every initiative believing that a bird in the hand was more valuable than the proverbial bird in the bush. While the good people stood by and didn't protest, protect or interfere, the criminals set about stealing everything that was not nailed down or closely guarded. As fast as Myrie bought truckloads of lumber and materials to build the furniture, most of it would disappear within a week. He brought all the machinery from Kingston, and it was quickly broken by carelessness. When he was present, the people he hired worked diligently, but when he was absent, they went to work on their ground but continued to collect a salary from Mr. Myrie. And so, the business became a leaking faucet that drained his resources.

Garnett complained bitterly that he was not able to be everywhere at the same time and supervise everything himself. "I feel like a one legged man in an ass kicking contest." He couldn't keep up and had no reliable employees on who he could depend. Even his trusted friends and relatives betrayed him by selling some of the materials he brought for the business.

He had arranged for a store in Kingston to take all the furniture he could produce but he could never meet the supply quota agreed on. While his workers were not themselves malicious or unkind by nature, they only looked out for their self-interest. But enlightened self-interest should have taught them that if Garnett succeeded, the entire community would have succeeded. While his house was ably built and stands as a monument to his success, he eventually had to abandon all his Woodlands business initiatives as even the television sets, his satellite dish, china, and silverware were stolen from his house when he was away. Within a year, he had run out of money. While he tried to convince them that they were all standing on the door of plenty if they wanted to work hard and were faithful to the cause, he felt defeated, disappointed, and frustrated with the "See and blind, hear and deaf" mentality that was embraced by the people.

This was detrimental to the entire community and to his business interests in particular. He abandoned his initiatives and got a job in Kingston while the twenty employees he had hired, and their dependents returned to scavenging for their daily plate of food.

On the many occasions when he visited Carolyn, he told her that distance and time away only made his heart grow fonder and how she was always on his mind wherever he roamed. He graphically told of his exploits in Africa that were difficult and comfortless, but more importantly, he talked about his ambition for the two of them now that he was back in Jamaica. The gentleman she was seeing not only stepped aside when he heard that Garnett was back, he left town and was not available even when Carolyn sent a message for him to visit her.

Carolyn was flattered by Garnett's attentions and devoured his stories. His strange and dangerous adventures were received with awe and admiration often punctuated with, "A wha you saying to me? Fi true?" By his bedside account to Carolyn, sometimes with her parents listening outside the door, he revealed to them that Dr. Rodney was able to obtain scholarships to all his faithful disciples from Jamaica to study in Cuba. Since Garnett was a wanted man in Jamaica for being a "trouble maker" and specifically to answer charges relating to his role in the riots, he decided to take up Dr. Rodney's invitation.

The arrangements for him to relocate to Cuba were made secretly through a Cuban agent in 1970. Then finally, on the appointed day in 1971, Garnett was told to pack a small bag with clothes and personal items and take the Ferry from Victoria Pier in Kingston to Port Royal. When he alighted from the Ferry and gave the prearranged signal placing his arm over his eyes as if he was hiding his eyes from the sun, he was met by a another Cuban gentleman and taken to the Royal Jamaican Yacht Club where he boarded a private yacht that met a large ship about five miles out to sea that then transported him to Havana. This was his first time away from Jamaica and he thought it might be the last time he would see his family, Woodlands, and Carolyn. As the cloud-crowned Blue Mountains receded from view, he thought there must be a million mountains in the world, but none that could be more beautiful.

He met several other Jamaicans as well as recruits from several countries, San Salvador, Nicaragua, Chili, Argentina, Granada, and Brazil. He spent a wonderful time with his mentor, Dr. Walter Rodney, who introduced him to Dr. Maurice Bishop who would become famous for attempting a takeover of Granada that was abruptly halted by President Ronald Reagan, using the United States Marine Corp, with the support of Prime Minister Edward Seaga and Eugenia Charles, president of Dominica. Dr. Rodney was subsequently assassinated in 1980 after he finally returned to Guyana to compete for political leadership.

In Cuba, Garnett was apprehensive but at the same time awed. Here was a place where there was work and bread for all; everyone could read and write and got free health care. He felt at home in his own skin. When he compared the quality fo life in Cuba to Jamaica, he couldn't deny the truth and lamented that it was not the slave mentality of Jamaica he left behind. Garnett lamented that it was as if Jamaicans continued to wear the same clothes that they wore when they were ten years old. He asked Dr. Rodney Jamaica would ever get over its "browning" obsession. Do you think black people can get justice from Jamaican judges who still wear the wigs of our slave masters?

He greatly admired Cubans for true heroism, unselfishness, and devotion to high ideals as well as their effort to put an end to poverty through education. He enthusiastically bought into Castro's "rigid conscience of duty and discipline" manifesto.

Garnett and the other recruits were inducted into the Cuban Army in 1971. For a year, he received training from Daniel Alarcon Ramfrez (Benigno) in hand to hand combat, to use hand guns, machine guns, surface to air missiles, bombs, grenades, and bayonets. When he became an expert, he felt like a killing machine. He was taught to camouflage himself with tree limbs and leaves as well as burry himself in the ground. He was being prepared to support himself in the jungle, how to prepare snakes and insects for dinner, find honey in trees, use chew sticks to clean his teeth, to stay physically fit and do first aid and minor surgery for himself and his comrades. He was in good spirits during his ordeal because he was so well treated and respected by his comrades as well as the Angolan people. He wanted to be like Chi Guevara, just a "Rootsman" who could adjust to whatever was required. He was articulate and fearless. Because of his fitness and endurance mixed with his concern for his fellow man, some of the Cubans nick-named him, "Lord Myrie, the soulful Christian preacher."

Agostino Neto, the leader of the Popular Movement for the Liberation of Angola (MPLA), who Chi Guevara befriended after they met in 1964 and promised that if he ever wanted help to just ask, finally asked for Cuba's help. Chi had encouraged Castro to support the ambitions of Neto to free his country from Portuguese colonial domination and poverty.

And so, in 1973, Garnett was one of the first two hundred guerilla fighters to be airlifted to a remote airfield built by the Cuban advisors near Luanda, and transported by trucks to one of the "Centros de Instruccion Revolucionaria" (CIR) for orientation. He was part of the advance forces so that on 4

November 1975, Neto and Castro could launch an intervention on an unprecedented scale. The mission was code-named "Operation Carlota" in honor of the leader of a slave rebellion in Cuba in 1843. Garnett was joined by about thirty thousand other guerilla fighters in support of the MPLA. Before being loaded onto the plane, Fidel Castro personally hugged each soldier, kissed him twice and pleaded with all of them to respect local customs and religious practices, exercise self-control, and in particular forbid them from having sexual contact with the women they encountered.

Castro's expressed objectives to the fighters was to "destroy colonial domination." This meant, not only expelling the Portuguese who had occupied Angola since the fifteenth century when they profited greatly from the slave trade, but also destroying the South African and Rhodesian Armies. Castro personally hated them for their apartheid policies. Finally, Castro was bent on defeating the FNLA (National Front for the Liberation of Angola) whose leaders were Mr. Holden Roberto and Mr. Jonas Savimbi, who lead the UNITA (National Union for the Total Independence of Angola). Both of these groups were heavily supported by Britain and the United States.

In Angola, it was always a good day for dangerous work. The South Africans were ruthless, brutal and unforgiving. If they found that someone from a village had betrayed them, they would kill every man jack, (73) and burn everything standing. Sometimes, his fear of being killed caused Garnett's heart to beat louder than the frequent explosions of guns. During the war, no one was kind to captors who were usually killed on the spot or severely injured so that it would require the attention of the victim's colleagues and distract them from the war effort.

The last campaign in which he participated was the Cuba-MPLA battle against their adversaries in Nshila wa Lufu called the Death Road, which produced heavy losses but also a decisive victory for the Cuba-MPLA forces in which they prevailed in all their objectives. Portugal (Estado Novo government), Rhodesia and South Africa were all defeated and withdrew from Angola. This prompted the rapid exodus of three hundred thousand Portuguese citizens called the "Retornados" who were hastily evacuated back to Portugal with planes provided by European countries. It was the dawn of a new era as the days of colonial rule was over for Angola!

As the United States had their hands full with Viet Nam, Castro was able to help his friend, Agostinho Neto and the MPLA form a government on their Independence Day, November 11, 1975. Castro generously provided advisors, teachers, doctors and technicians from 1976 onward. After Neto died from a heart attack on September 10, 1979, Mr. Jose dos Santos succeeded him. Equality and democracy had taken root.

Garnett told Carolyn that it was absolutely hell over there. A half a million soldiers and civilians were killed during these conflicts but that he had come through the fire and survived to return to Jamaica in 1976—mission accomplished! He repeated to himself, "Mi hard man fi dead."

Garnett had no difficulty blending in with the local people. While he was fully armed, he disguised himself as one of the locals and adopted their dress, language and manner. It was a great advantage to be indistinguishable from the people for whom he was fighting. The people bought into the struggle and gave him and his fellow fighter's food, shelter, intelligence on enemy locations and came to his rescue on numerous occasions. Since he was fighting the cruel and licentious South African and Rhodesian Armies, he told Carolyn that he reflected on the Nyabinghi sessions he attended in Kingston in Mortimo Planno's yard that always opened with, "Death to the White man." While these were empty curses, it was an amazing experience to have had a license and even a duty to kill any and all white men on sight. It was kill or be killed and he got very good at it. He often laughed to himself that many people were "talking" about changing the apartheid policies in South African but here he was, a country boy from Woodlands District, on the front line ambushing and killing every South African, Rhodesian or Portuguese he encountered.

During the Guerrilla fighting, he learned he had a great capacity to adapt and endure. "In addition to never being at the mercy the enemy who were trying to kill me or worst, I focused on the three essentials of survival in Angola: water, food, and shelter." The skills he learned growing up in Woodlands climbing coconut and mango trees, running errands, living in the woods and learning what was edible and what was not proved invaluable. On one occasion, he insisted that his colleagues sleep tied to the limbs of tall trees but most of them did not follow his advice. The South Africans attacked as soon as the sun came up and he awoke to gunshots that slaughtered all the men who slept on the ground. As they could not reveal their position in the trees, the dozen men who followed his advice waited and were then able to track the South Africans and kill them all in a surprise attack before returning to evacuate their fallen comrades.

Carolyn was stirred by his war stories and intently listened to his extravagant narratives that were worth the telling as well as the hearing. Garnett told her that while the Cuban-led fighters traveled in convoys of thirty soldiers with five officers, and mostly lived in tents, they were expected to support themselves from the charity of the Ovimbundu and Ambudu people or by stealing food and water wherever they found it. That too, was a skill learned in Woodlands stealing fruit. He learned to catch rainwater in his helmet and transferred it to his water bottles and even to extract water from swamps with the handkerchief he always carried. He also learned to clean his body with alcohol swipes. He fought bravely and his commander Harry "Pombo" Villegas as well as President Neto personally gave him high praise testifying to his courage under fire. Angola now existed in fact.

Garnett thought to himself how independence brought tangible changes in the lives of the people in Angola unlike the semblance of Independence in Jamaica that only benefited the rich and brought no change or improvement in the lives of the masses and economic prosperity continued to be denied black people who on the most part remained illiterate and continued to beg for their daily bread while most of the land belonged to estates. Jamaica had independence but most of the people could still not aspire to become a justice of the peace or a judge, a rank higher than sergeant in the police or the defense force. Although everyone obtained universal suffrage in 1944 and could vote, elections were manipulated to keep ten per cent in power. Several public parks were restricted to the majority of the people—based on skin color.

While he received no recognition from politicians, he was satisfied with the respect and affection he was receiving from Carolyn as well as the people of Woodlands. Because Carolyn was a good Christian girl who was expected to retain her virginity until she was married, no intimacy had existed between them. But one lonely night he was in Woodlands struggling and even trembling with delusions of the passion between them and feeling the need for female companionship, he drove to Brighton with sinful fire in his belly to see the love of his life. He parked the car several chains away and walked on stone steps in the soft moonlight through the cane piece with the long leaves brushing against his face and excitedly tapped on Carolyn's wooden bedroom window. She opened it and was glad to see him. He quickly climbed in and was in a sweet embrace when her father came to her door and demanded to know who was in her room.

Carolyn tried to push him out of the window but although embarrassed by the lack of dignity in the situation he said, "No

Sah, mi no mek no man run me. Open the door." So Carolyn opened the door and her father told Garnett that visitors to his home usually use the front door and declared in no uncertain terms that he was no longer welcome in his house. "Mr. Dennis, with all due respect Sah, mi love you daughter and want to marry her." Her father, who knew about Garnett's chronic womanizing, replied, "So you plan to marry mi daughter. Let me ask you a simple straight forward question: Can you promise me and her that you will give up all your women and be faithful only to her?" Garnett swallowed his spit even though his mouth was already dry and told Carolyn that he already had two children and he was not going to lie, "As a Jamaican man, I don't believe I could stop seeing other women even under the best of circumstances." Carolyn then responded, "Garnett, as much as I love you, I don't think we can have a life together." Her father then said, "Mr. Myrie, I have nothing against you but I oppose the marriage because you are not a one woman man and you would only end up making mi daughter miserable. Good night sir."

So, things did not turn out the way he imagined. So he humbly high tailed it back to his car with a deflated ego and made his way to Woodlands as a poor, frustrated and unfortunate creature. The feeling of dishonor, loneliness and embarrassment was enormous. He ended up at the house of his father's old flame with which he regularly and repeatedly had sexual intercourse. She was only too glad to accommodate him and she took the opportunity to show him the sleeping child that his father had fathered and who was now thirteen years old. She told him that life was a drab with most of the men she liked had gone to England and there was no more joy and happiness in Woodlands. He enjoyed the night food that she offered that went a long way to restore his pride and dignity but did not come close to satisfy his longing. After making it back to his parent's house and sleeping it off, he made his way to Kingston the next day brokenhearted.

In the ensuing five years, he would have no contact with Carolyn and neither of them found true love with anyone else. Then just as she was about to board a city bus to make her way home from her teaching duties, she heard a voice, "Chickie, don't mount the bus!" It was the voice of her long lost love. She turned from the bus, grinning with excitement, waved at him, ran back down the platform against the flow of the embarking passengers, met his open arms and hugged him with a determination that almost suffocated both of them. She then parted her lips to receive the kiss she had longed for.

Carolyn had grown to detest both men and boys who were too cautious, fretful and who constantly worried about life's insecurities and dangers. She called them "fraidy, fraidy men."

She was always remembering how fearless and manly Garnett was and comparing them to him. So she confessed to him, "I have been miserable and wanted to find you. Everywhere I go, I search the crowd looking for your face and longing for a moment like this." He told her that there will never be another woman for him. As low as his spirits were, he was much pleased and immediately felt cheered and refreshed. From that faithful day, their hearts regained their joy and they were committed to each other. They spent the evening over a wonderful meal that she prepared at her house in Portmore, caught up on what each were doing over the past five years, laughing and delighting in each other's company. They were both now twenty-nine years old.

After dinner and much conversation about their individual lives, he wanted her and she was finally willing. In her bedroom, she surrendered to their needs. He found her body beautiful and inviting. He had obsessed about her for all his adult life and she was finally naked in his arms and in the rapture of their love. Her cries of pleasure were loud and agreeable. In fact, she repeated "yes" over and over until she changed it to, "Oh my god," "Oh my god," "Oh my god" as if in fervent prayer. She held onto him with tears of happiness mixed in with sweat. It was a special moment until he ruined it by saying, "That's how mi luv fi sweat!" She pushed him away and hurried to wrap a robe around her naked body. He grabbed her arm and pulled her back to the bed. "Mi no done wid you yet!" She felt ravaged. She felt conflicted, however, because at some level, she believed that what she was doing was wicked and shameful. Her parents had beat into her that lust is evil and would lead to destruction. "Chicken merry, hawk de near." But in this moment, she put it out of her mind. Her long lost love had come back into her life at last.

During their five year absence from each other, while his big house in Woodlands stood like a monument unoccupied except for his younger brother (Joshie) looking after it for him, all his business plans for Woodlands failed. He even bought three trucks and haul materials all over Jamaica but ended up working for Vanguard Security from 1977 to 1981. He was terminated when he failed to provide sufficient security and allowed a shipment of ganja on an Air Jamaica flight to New York. This became an international incident.

The perpetrators had set off a bomb in another part of the airport that created a diversion and he had left his post unguarded to investigate and unwittingly allowed the shipment of ganja on the plane. He was also fired from another security job at Global Security in 1983 when he was caught promoting his own business on company time. He had come up with the idea of doing undercover work to identify who was stealing from companies and was able to hire people to go underground and foil these robberies. His early successes and his reputation increased the demand for his services but he was not ready to leave his employment when someone showed one of his business cards to his employer and he was immediately terminated. He was now forced to rely on running his own undercover business fulltime and it proved to be a success.

One of the innovations he brought back from Cuba was his night goggles. He enjoyed dressing in black and strapping on his goggles and watching the night-time activities in his neighborhood without being detected. He was particularly successful in using these goggles to identify people who were stealing from the various business interests that contracted for his services. His undercover work got results and several of the thieves who were caught red handed puzzled as to how Mr. Myrie could see in the dark.

Through hard work and ambition, Carolyn obtained a masters degree from the University of the West Indies and was the Principal of an elementary school. She told Garnett that she was not going to require that he be faithful to her as she knew that he could never live up to that promise. She had heard too many stories of other families, who, unknown to wives, showed up at funerals claiming that their husbands had other families, as well as meeting other women in hospitals claiming to be wives of the patient. Carolyn decided that she would rather know the truth than to play the game of "willful ignorance."

In anticipation of the pleasures of a happy home, within a week, they had set a date for their marriage. With this new commitment, he wrote to his parents in England with the good news as well as made their way to Brighton and Woodlands to visit family and friends all for the sake of finally receiving their family's blessings. But several of Carolyn's family, suspicious of the source of his wealth and his womanizing, tried to impede their impending union. "He will leave you with pickney and no support." Aunt Beryl, on the other hand, was delighted with the news and started making plans for the wedding immediately. She adored Carolyn. His promise to all who doubted him as marriage material was, "I don't drink, I don't smoke and I don't go a road." It was not by accident that he left out any mention of his other women who he continued to see even as his marriage plans were being made.

He had one of the diamonds that he had brought back from Angola made into an engagement ring and, inspired by his deep thoughts, wrote a poem for the occasion. As he was visiting her after she was already prepared for sleep, he sat on a chair beside her bed and recited by heart, "Chickie Sweetheart, Darling, the love I have to offer you is pure and strong. It has nothing of false intention to lull you with lies or elusion. I want to see you happy, completely happy—in a settling frame of quality. And I believe you are too sincere to reject my offer. I want to see you free, basically free from unconscious conflict. And today, once again, I offer my love to you that will lead us to matrimony. Will you marry me?"

She was impressed, but she was much too practical to get mushy and sentimental, "Garnett, cut the bull shit, I have no illusions that marrying you is going to be easy. Against the advice of my family, I agree to marry you because mi weak fi yu. But I am going to fasten my seatbelt because I know it's going to be a bumpy ride. If you receive me as I am with all my deficiencies and misguided opinions, I will receive you as you are as well." So he placed the diamond ring on her finger and she lifted the sheet that covered her body and invited Garnett to take off his clothes and join her.

The ecstasy was beyond description. With his head pillowed between her breasts, they spent the rest of the night and the following day in bed. They had finally found each other and were happy. Their life grew happier with each passing day. He was now her man and she accommodated herself in every way to his needs and preferences. When he visited her obviously reeking of the other woman's odor, she asked him, "Were you with another woman?" His answer was "Yes. And you are next. If you take care of the banana, the banana will take care of you."

They married on the twenty-second of August 1983 at the Richmond Park Moravian Church with the Rev. Justin Peart presiding. While her father continued to harbor doubts about Carolyn's decision, she was now thirty, living on her own and could make her own decisions. Many an eye was blurred with tears of happiness as she vowed to celebrate each anniversary and recall these happy memories each year without regret. The beautiful wedding was followed by a reception at Devon House where the wine and spirits flowed. The food was delicious. Joshie was happy and exclaimed, "Mi Belly full and mi heart full!" The congratulatory speeches went on much too long as usual. There were so many unsteady feet trying to dance that one guest even suggested that the only difference between a Jamaican wedding and a Jamaican funeral was one less drunk. His parents came all the way from England and his older Brother Patrick who had migrated to the United States came back for the occasion. It was a fine family reunion for many people who had not seen each other for a long time. Their union produced two children.

In Angola, he was a professional soldier doing a job. Now that he was basking in Carolyn's love, he learned he could be a warm and loving man, a man capable of jealousy, greed, vanity, and fear. He learned to enjoy the simple meals she prepared, laugh at the silly things she did and the jokes she told. She was forever playful and he relaxed and was always good natured around her. He was particularly amused when she opened her hope chest and saw the fine linens, napkins, sheets, pillow cases, Wedgewood dishes, silver knives, spoons and forks and the furnishings she had put aside over the years for her marital home. She was just as happy to finally empty their contents.

He felt happy even when there was nothing to be happy about. He was a master at retaining Carolyn's affection despite the many lies he told her. Even though he was married, with his unquenchable thirst for sex, he equated his ability to father many children as a testament to his manhood. After all, Bob Marley had thirteen, Peter Tosh had ten and another member of the Wailers fathered over fifty. They fathered practically all the children with other women while married. He would use her, deceive and betray her time and again. But her forgiving heart never belabored what she found out. She chose to ignore all the whispers and reports she received about other women. Tomorrow was another day.

So, Carolyn became a great influence on Garnett as she insisted on doing the right thing in business as well as in their family and social relationships. Working together, MICA Security flourished. They had one thousand employees ten years later. Many were hired from Woodlands District.

Carolyn's constant refrain to Garnett was hustling and lying will only get you somewhere for a little while, let's build a business and a life for the long term. As a concession to her, he always thought through the long term impact of whatever he was thinking of doing.

He discovered five amazing truths: (1) a clean conscience is a wonderful thing; (2) winning in the long run requires integrity; (3) it was much easier to be honorable and kind with a good bank account; (4) to get the full value out of life, you must have family and friends to share your success. He had a good laugh when the thought came to him: (5) It is not the love of money that tempts men to be dishonest, it's the lack of money!

Carolyn is often characterized as a Christian unselfish woman, forgiving of those who err, offering succor for the distressed and full of generous impulses. She has room in her heart for all the bruised and abused children who knock on her door. Readily admitting that her marriage is unconventional, she is fond of quoting the poem by Isaac Watts:

> "LET dogs delight to bark and bite,
> For God hath made them so;
> Let bears and lions growl and fight,
> For 't is their nature to".

I love my husband unconditionally. He is who he is and I love him just the way he is. I resolved before I married him, not to become the sucking wife as other women had done worrying and trying to control their men when Jamaican men cannot help themselves." On the other hand, she has remained the faithful devoted wife, mother, and business partner.

Garnett continued to be the man of few restraints as he entertained his guests with a ready wit and an appreciation for what he fancied was good living. He never denied his twelve outside children and always took an active part in their upbringing. Carolyn also never complained about her husband's lust for other women as well as fathering children outside their marriage. In fact, they are all welcome in her home from time to time.

Chapter III

And the Band Played On

Mr. Myrie was large and in charge. They found their stride and the business was a success. With his increasing wealth, he lived off the fat of the land, enjoyed the company of beautiful women, ate and drank frequently and no longer did any physical work. His employees debated whether sex was ninety per cent work and ten per cent fun or the opposite. They decided that if it was ninety per cent work, Mr. Myrie would hire someone to do it for him as he now got in the habit of ordering someone else to do the work—even to move a coffee cup from his desk back to the kitchen. His weight increased and his stamina decreased. He was too busy for exercise and now had to take time to deal with disease.

He started waking up frequently at night to pass urine and often felt fatigued. Mrs. Myrie insisted that he go to the doctor where they learned that he had advanced diabetes. The doctor said it could have been avoided if he had eaten less and exercised more. So a strict diet and exercise regimen was ordered. He took one look at the recommended foods and said, "So the only way to be healthy is to eat what I don't want, drink what don't taste good and waste my time exercising." He found it difficult and inconvenient to take his insulin shots on schedule, go out for the prescribed morning walks and to eat less, so his diabetes worsened. He became blind and because the sores on his legs caused by him bumping and falling over things, refused to heal he was frequently despondent. "How mi guan find time to run mi business and exercise?"

While he feared no man, diabetes would drive him deeper into iniquity. The amount of money for eye surgery, medications, and visits to the doctor, staying in hospitals, full time chauffer and housekeeper had him complaining that he was spending more money than he was making. To maintain his health, he was spending all his time and money in the health care system and left him lacking the ambition to climb mountains, navigate oceans or cross desserts. He was just relieved to lift the covers each morning and not see a tag on one of his big toes.

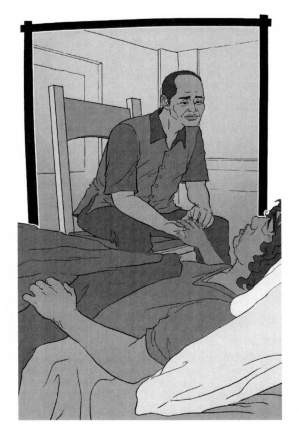

In 1998, Garnett received word that his ninety-six-year-old granny was on her deathbed. He left a business meeting he was chairing to immediately go to Woodlands and was at her bedside when she admonished him about his womanizing but blessed him as well as his brothers. With a final deep breath, she was gone. It was a great sadness for him. As people in Woodlands believed that when people died, they get to personally meet with God about others left behind, there was plenty of people at the house asking if there was anything they could do to help and particularly to get word to Zerefa to give a good report to God when she gets home so God will send them a special blessing. Sick people were always treated with kindness as a testimonial of their virtue with an expectation of a reward. Duppy have power.

Woodlands people all believe that death is a journey of the soul from this world to a better place where there is no pain or sorrow. It was always a curiosity to Garnett that a land of milk and honey with angels flying about was the best the church could come up with to motivate the living to do God's will. He would joke that he always preferred the company of bad women than the boring well-behaved people who think they are on the road to heaven.

As soon as the death of his Grandmother was reported to Minister Craig, the bell ringer was asked to toll the large bell in the belfry at Springfield Moravian Church that was pulled by a long rope. The toiling continued for one hour calling the entire community to gather at the home of the deceased to pay respects to and comfort the bereaved. Within a few hours, fifty people gathered. Some of the women washed and anointed the body with coconut oil as well as dressed her for the viewing and the men obtained the dimensions the body to make the coffin and dig the deep six foot grave (east and west) in the family plot.

Garnett contracted with Brown's Funeral Home in Black River to take charge of the remaining details and they took the corpse from the house feet first. The most common thing that Garnett heard as people talked to each other as, "Ask not for whom the bell tolls, it tolls for you and me." He thought to himself how philosophical people become when they are reminded of their mortality.

In addition to covering mirrors in the house, wearing only black and white clothes, turning the bed mattress against the wall and rearranging the furniture, passing of a baby over the corpse three times, swept and cleaned the entire house. Some of the women immediately started cooking in washed out ten gallon kerosene cans. The white rum would help to drown out their sorrow as well as quench the thirst of those assembled. For the following nine nights, the community gathered to keep vigil with the family, pray, play dominoes, sing and dance (kumina or Kete style) with tambourines. They cried, laughed, told duppy stories, relive and praise the life of the dearly departed.

While men were restrained from showing much emotion, some of the old men who had known Zerefa all her life cried quietly while several women wailed. Garnett never did understand the nine night tradition so his mother, who was now on good terms with Garnett and had returned from England, told him that the "set up" custom started because they didn't want to make a mistake and bury a person who was not dead so they would wait nine nights to give the person every opportunity to wake up. Lots of noise was made in an effort to wake the dead. A second reason is to ward off evil spirits and assure that the recently departed soul is not prevented by the devil from her ascension into heaven.

As Garnett was a successful businessman and took charge, contrary to what was customary, no one felt the need to help with the tremendous cost of the food, drinks, and materials for the funeral. In addition to curry goat and rice and curry chicken, Garnett ordered that a cow be butchered. For the carpenters, grave diggers, the women who prepared the food and the body for burial, this was ordinarily a labor of love and no one expected to be paid except Garnett filled their outstretched hands.

The number of songs at the wake was endless and as most people could not read, Raypet, the song leader, called out the next line of a song for everyone else to follow. The favorite nine night songs were:

"Mi sah mi ole man dead and he no lef no will; He lef a likkle piece of land fi feed the whole a we; but mi bigger breda tief it way from wi; glory be to God, glory be to God fi de whole a wi."

"Adam in the garden hide himself, hide himself, hide himself; Adam in the garden hide himself, hide himself from God". And finally, they would sing every verse of "You have longed for sweet peace":

You have longed for sweet peace, and for faith to increase,
And have earnestly, fervently prayed;
But you cannot have rest, or be perfectly blest,
Until all on the altar is laid.

Is your all on the altar of sacrifice laid?
Your heart, does the Spirit control?
You can only be blest and have peace and sweet rest,
As you yield Him your body and soul.

Would you walk with the Lord in the light of His Word,
And have peace and contentment alway;
You must do His sweet will to be free from all ill;
On the altar your all you must lay.

Oh, we never can know what the Lord will bestow
Of the blessings for which we have prayed,
Till our body and soul He doth fully control,
And our all on the altar is laid.

Who can tell all the love He will send from above!
Oh, how happy our heart will be made!
Oh, what fellowship sweet we shall share at His feet,
When our all on the altar is laid!

Elisha Albright Hoffman (1839-1929) Music: Elisha Albright Hoffman (1839-1929)

After the ninth night, the coffin was brought from the funeral home in a black limousine to the church. The entire community attended with men dressed in black suits and the women in white dresses and offered their testimonials emphasizing what a God fearing woman she was. Everyone, young, old, were encouraged to give a testimony. The choir sang, the minister preached and prayed, and the family wept. The women of the church provided fans and held members of the family in kind embraces as needed. The attentiveness of friends kept grieving family members from hurting themselves when they inevitably fainted.

After the service, the six pallbearers picked up the coffin and took it to the hearse and started a parade to the burial site with everyone singing as they walked. A second service took place at the grave where the minister reminded all who were in attendance, "Dust to dust, ashes to ashes is the way of all flesh. Soon and very soon, we all have appointments to see the King." The coffin was placed over the grave and finally lowered to the bottom with Zerefa to face the rising sun though eternity. The two ropes used to lower the body into the grave were pulled out after the coffin came to rest. Several people would say, "Good bye Zerefa, see you soon." Some mourners took some of the grave dirt and with their backs turned to the grave throw it into the grave between their legs.

The final song of farewell was "How great Thou Art." (Carrie Underwood)

O Lord my God, When I in awesome wonder,
Consider all the worlds Thy Hands have made;
I see the stars, I hear the rolling thunder,
Thy power throughout the universe displayed.

Then sings my soul, my Savior God, to Thee,
How great Thou art, How great Thou art.
Then sings my soul, my Saviour God, to Thee,
How great Thou art, How great Thou art!

When through the woods, and forest glades I wander,
And hear the birds sing sweetly in the trees.
When I look down, from lofty mountain grandeur
And see the brook, and feel the gentle breeze.

Then sings my soul, my Saviour God, to Thee,
How great Thou art, How great Thou art.
Then sings my soul, my Saviour God, to Thee,
How great Thou art, How great Thou art!

And when I think of God, His Son not sparing;
Sent Him to die, I scarce can take it in;
That on the Cross, my burden gladly bearing,
He bled and died to take away my sin.

Then sings my soul, my Saviour God, to Thee,
How great Thou art, How great Thou art.
Then sings my soul, my Saviour God, to Thee,
How great Thou art, How great Thou art!

When Christ shall come, with shout of acclamation,
And take me home, what joy shall fill my heart.
Then I shall bow, in humble adoration,
And then proclaim, "My God, how great Thou art!"

Then sings my soul, my Saviour God, to Thee,
How great Thou art, How great Thou art.
Then sings my soul, my Saviour God, to Thee,
How great Thou art, How great Thou art!

No one left before the last shovel of dirt was tossed and then wondered back to the house to partake of the abundant virtuals that Garnett provided. During the feast, family and friends reflected on something Zerefa repeatedly said before she died, "I do not want to be looking all over heaven for my family so you must live a good life with clean hands and a pure heart so you can all be with me in paradise."

A burial is a serious matter in Woodlands as overlooking some minute detail may vex the duppy and subject a family to a lifetime of haunts and torments if the duppy decide to take up residence in one's home in the form of a family pet. Evidence that this has occurred is the persistent mewing of the cat or the howling of a dog. Cows and duppys keep company and keep each other's secrets. Cows can become duppies in the form of rolling calfs dragging their chain when duppies take over the cow. So to avoid these developments, the family must nail the dearly departed hand and foot. The sleeves of the dress and the heel of the socks were nailed to the coffin. The people who lived a good life would be buried east to west but criminals and bad men would be buried north-south. For hardened criminals who had killed others, they were "planted" head first with their feet to the sky. But if all else fails and the family residence is now haunted, the Obeahman must be called to take off the duppy—for a price.

At the reception following the funeral Mass Bertie pointed out that once upon a time, people lived forever. There were no births and no deaths. But the people asked God to give them children and He said that would only be possible if people would also accept death. They unanimously agreed and so it was that every time a child is born, someone dies. In Woodlands District, invariably the news of a death was accompanied by news of a birth and sure enough, word came that Mrs. Eva Smith had given birth to a bouncing baby girl.

Even with his diminished health from diabetes, Garnett maintained an active interest in politics. It can be an addictive preoccupation. With his work, his popularity and sensitivity to social problems, with the support for the People's National Party (PNP) in 2007, he finally decided to accept their nomination to be a Member of Parliament from North West St. Elizabeth.

His platform included addressing the blights that continued to adversely affect the people from the teachings of Dr. Rodney, a preventive program of social reform and giving poor people access to idle lands. Committing himself to closing the gap between the rich and poor, Garnett became known as the "antipoverty candidate" with his slogan, "No man without land and no land without men who want to work it."

In his acceptance speech he said, "The past fifty years in Jamaica have been characterized by glaring inequality, an active underground economy, high inflation, a weak currency, reduced incomes, high food and energy costs, inordinate influence of Dons and gangs along with flagrant disregard for law and order. Foreign investors are few and our professionals and entrepreneurs are leaving our country with their disposable wealth, knowledge and skills to seek their fortunes elsewhere. We cannot continue to ignore this turmoil.

Every society has people who live in the mainstream, who contribute to and hold a stake in the community; and others, who, by choice or circumstance, live on the margins. The "margins" of Jamaica have reached such proportions that they threaten to become the new mainstream. The rivers have swelled their banks, and the single most important factor in holding back the tide is rigorous enforcement of the rights to private property.

I asked someone who live in one of our extra legal communities how much his family of seven pays for rent, and he said they did not pay rent. I then asked who owned the house they lived in, and he said he didn't know but they have been living there for over twelve years. So how do you get electricity, water and sewage? "We just work it out."

It may seem like the cruelest of "proposals" to pin our hopes for social progress on private property, when any serious attempt to enforce private property in Jamaica would, in the short term, make outlaws out of a third of the population. But we do people who live on the margins no favors in allowing them to occupy land to which they have no claim.

The most important vehicle for social mobility is home ownership. For most of us it is the most important asset we will ever own. It is our address, our identity. It is literally the bedrock beneath our feet. We gain equity in it. We borrow against it to educate our children, address critical health issues for our loved ones and to start a business. With any luck, we bequeath it to our children and grandchildren.

The single most important source of funds for new business start up for various enterprises in developed countries is real estate (one's home). In spite of their obvious poverty, if we adopted a concerted approach to establish good title (legally enforceable property rights) for property occupied by the poor, we may find that we already have the assets to rescue the country and put us on a path to prosperity. At present, real estate taxes are collected on only a small portion of our land.

The energies and aspirations of the poor are waiting to be released. As much as 50 percent of our people are "coutching" in extralegal land. While the value of any given plot may not have high value, cumulatively, the value is substantial. The moment is ripe for action. Let us unleash the potential of these dead assets. There is a great deal of value in our land.

The first step is to update our records and to fix ownership to every parcel of land in a formally organized computerized system certifying each owner. By accomplishing this awesome task:

1. Property owners would be vested along with the owner's right to contract for water, telephone, sewage and electrical services as well as enhancing the value of our land holdings by increasing the net of potential numbers of buyers if and

when they decide to alienate (give away or sell) their land holdings.

2.   Debts could be more easily collected.

3.   Law enforcement would be facilitated.

4.   Taxes could be collected.

5.   A more accurate census could be taken that would enhance voter registration and extend voting rights to landless or homeless citizens.

6.   Delivery of mail, summons and service would be possible.

7.   Property owners would be motivated to form Homeowners Associations to enhance the value of their properties and protect value.

8.   Pride of ownership would be extended to more citizens.

9.   The need for bribing government officials and Dons would be greatly reduced.

Albert Einstein taught us that there is enough energy in a brick to make an atomic bomb that could destroy a city if we only had the skills to harness and release its energy. Likewise, there is substantial potential in these shacks and dead assets if we can draw out the value and convert them to real value. Dunns River may be a beautiful river but it also generates electricity that powers manufacturing and production.

Land reform can be the platform on which the entire economy can be based. As a primarily agrarian society, it could be a tremendous boost to the economy if it then leads to increased production as the price of food is increasing rapidly not only in Jamaica but in the world.

Over the past fifty years, there has been a steady increase of citizens moving from country to Kingston and Montego Bay. This was graphically depicted in the movie "The Harder They Come". When they arrive, legal and social barriers prevent them from acquiring legal housing, acquire training and education, obtain employment or start a business. They are more likely to work as day laborers or in the underground economy where they become easy victims of exploitation.

At tremendous cost to individuals as well as our country, our legal system is not only stacked against the poor, it is hostile. Rather than promoting the ambitions of its citizens, the poor are treated like criminals and our government purposely imposes rules and obstacles that serve to thwart their ability to make a living. We seem bent on finding a problem for every solution.

Establishing a legal business in Jamaica is a formidable business. Obtaining the right forms, filling them out, standing in lines, paying the fees and obtain the necessary certifications to operate is a long frustrating process requiring an investment of six months of red tape even if you are a sophisticated businessman. The cost is at least a year's pay for an average worker. Most people opt out of the system and operate their business illegally. In Jamaica, a citizen cannot open a bank account without a utility bill in the person's name. What is the hidden agenda for these rules?

As much as our people try to do the right thing, the rigidity and cumbersomeness of our laws breaks our citizens more than they break the law. They do clandestine work and apply creative ingenious survival strategies because, without a support system or a little handholding, these recent arrivals to the city are hopelessly reduced to living as outlaws—outside the legal system. Residents in these communities can pay someone to illegally register an automobile, buy their driver's license, buy groceries, get their automobiles repaired, visit barbershops and beauty salons, use taxis, purchase baked goods, obtain the services of a dentist who may have never graduated from dental school and pays no taxes. But there is a huge cost to bribe officers of the law and local "big men" for protection and the opportunity to operate their various enterprises. Even homeless boys who wash windscreens pay a Don a part of what they receive for the privilege. Paying taxes would actually cost less and would certainly be less intimidating. Working in the underground economy, they have tremendous competition with each other but they also have to fight the government. If the system is in conflict with the way our people live, we should not be surprised that frustration, discontent, corruption, disrespect for the law, poverty and violence is the predictable outcome. It takes cunning ginnals to outwit the system just to survive.

Government allocations are never for development, training, housing or education for extralegal communities. Whatever is budgeted by the government always take the form of control—police actions, clamping down, and catching criminals.

Properties change hands regularly as people get jobs and move. These transactions are not registered nor do not involve lawyers or the tax office. These sales (social contracts) are either cash sales or gifts with no transfer of recorded title. Even expensive properties are bought and sold accompanied by some public gathering where the announcement is made so that "everyone" knows whose property it is. The dogs know who their owners are and the limits of their property.

The downside is that these valuable assets are commercially and financially invisible because the people occupying the property has no indicia of ownership to take to the bank for a loan to start a business or purchase an automobile.

In addition to setting up an efficient court system to establish title, my proposal is to establish macroeconomic reform in Jamaica. Let us marshal the resources at our disposal to:

1. Correct this legal failure and create a unified system that is more conducive to a productive and dynamic market economy.

2. Properly survey, map, record all the land in our country and keep our records current and accurate.

3. Research the "chain of title" to include the rights of adverse possessors (squatters rights).

4. Establish a formal property system that integrates the reality of land ownership with the legal records that give good title to people who are rightful owners.

5. Establish the property rights of extra legals.

6. Assume that if land taxes have not been paid for seven years, the property has been abandoned. (Much of our land has been abandoned by people who migrate and no longer have an interest in the property they left behind or the owners may have died and their children have no ownership interest and have taken no steps to establish ownership, pay taxes or to alienate the property).

7. Since our government has a history of making straight roads crooked, we need to establish a ministry of advocacy or a nongovernment organization whose responsibility it is to do the following:

   a. Review our systems and streamline our bureaucracy to accommodate the needs of our citizens to become legal taxpaying entrepreneurs. (It is never enough to pass equitable laws without the will to implement them efficiently and painlessly in the social reality of our country. Laws and governments should serve the people).

b. Make a strong effort to communicate the advantages of becoming legal. They could, for example, openly operate and advertise their goods and services to a wider customer base.

c. A place to turn for those who are frustrated that they cannot negotiate the process of becoming legal.

d. Make these valuable assets commercially and financially visible.

Public animosity toward judges, attorney, and public officials as agents of the rich could be greatly reduced. When most people obey and support the law, it is easy to enforce it against the few who break the law. But if most people break the law, it is impossible to enforce them, and everyone can do what they want to do with impunity. Property ownership is the single most important ingredient for instilling respect for the law. According to Lyndon Johnson, past president of the United States, "We can only have a law abiding society if everyone has a stake in it." Countries with wide distribution of land ownership are stable, prosperous, discourage unruly behavior, and respect for the rights of others increase.

By integrating current extra-legals into our legal system, we will release the aspirations and energies of poor people by giving them a stake in the country that they will want to protect. It is time for custom and social contracts to be integrated and come under the umbrella of the formal law. This is a win, win, win for all concerned. As Jamaicans travel and learn how other societies are organized for prosperity, their frustration and bitterness will grow. On the other hand, this plan will liberate the poor and prepare them to be citizens qualified to participate in the development of the country.

The people liked his platform and applauded him wherever he spoke. It was expensive for him personally, but he wanted it. He was popular, spoke well and ahead in the polls when the fifteen-year-old daughter of his family's housekeeper told the police that Mr. Myrie had fondled her. Even as the girl's mother swore that her daughter was lying, Garnett was arrested and charged with sexually assaulting the girl. The charges were dropped after the girl came out of hiding and confessed that someone paid her to lie and refused to go to court. But Garnett had already sacrificed himself for the good of the party, even though Paul Burke (one of the stalwarts in the PNP) and all of his supporters encouraged him to stay in the race and issued the following statement, "I shall continue to support Mr. Myrie. I do not believe this accusation and I am certain he is not guilty." Garnett knew that politics was a dirty business.

As the years passed, he grew to be a homebody, gentler, more considerate, and more committed to his wife of twenty-five years. Their silver anniversary was a merry one, lavishly presented at the Pegasus Hotel in New Kingston on August 30, 2008. There were endless testimonials from the two hundred family, friends, business associates and political colleagues—including Prime Minister Portia Simpson Miller, all his children and some of their mothers. They all signaled their veneration to this very complex man and his loyal wife.

After a wonderful meal of salad, curry goat, curry chicken, escovitch fish, rice and peas, corn pone and rum punch, it finally came time for the speech from the Big Man. So he was introduced by the eloquent Ms. Claudett Genas who told of the many public service awards from the PNP and most notably being selected as one of the fifty most outstanding citizens in the history of St. Elizabeth, "In addition to his family, the bad boy of Woodlands became the King of Woodlands and a valued friend to many. He continues to spend a great deal of time and resources trying to improve the lives of people throughout Jamaica. He is notorious throughout the country for his many kindnesses and his good works. Ladies and Gentlemen, a good friend is better than pocket money. Put your hands together and welcome to the podium, Mr. Garnett Myrie." Resplendent in his red tie, he rose and was assisted to the microphone by his wife.

"Good night and thank you for coming. I hope you have enjoyed your supper. I have certainly enjoyed the wonderful compliments that so many of you showered on both of us. I stand before you a broken man—half the man I used to be. I am blind. I am constantly falling over things and hurting myself. I get by with lots of help from my wife, my children, and the many people who still love me even though they have every reason not to.

I have indulged myself in a totally selfish life doing whatever I pleased without any thought of how much harm and pain I left in my wake. I have exercised no impulse control. I hurt the people that I cared about the most. So I want to take the opportunity to publicly apologize to my wife for the sleepless nights and pain I have caused her. Carolyn, you are the strongest and most sensible person I know. I now feel ashamed of myself. I was a deceiver and a liar. I take full responsibility. I am sorry for not being more responsible. Let me also use this occasion to specifically apologize to all my children, the other mothers of my children, my employees, all of you who were victims of my overindulgence. I take the blame and ask for your forgiveness. I see things differently as I get older. As Jimmy Cliff would say: "I can see clearly now that I am blind." I wish all the young men of Jamaica would resist their urges and dedicate themselves to one love. When they don't it has severe consequences for all concerned, especially for the children. I was born with teeth so I snarl and bite and play the dog.

I celebrate the fact that I believe you and I were born at the greatest time in the history of the world. As Jamaica did not have a radio station until 1959, growing up without even a radio, I marvel at the invention of television, FAX machines, computers, cell phones and the internet. We enjoyed the exploits of Bob Marley, Peter Tosh, Tiger Woods, the Williams Sisters, Chris Gale, Usain Bolt, the "Pocket Rocket" (Shelley Ann Frazier) Barack Obama, and the first woman prime minister of Jamaica. "We love you, Sistah P." I pity anyone who was not fortunate to be born a Jamaican.

In the time I have left on this world, if I have treated any of you badly, I would like to make it up to you. To my wife, I looked high and low for the perfect gift, so I hope this gold and diamond Rolex watch will remind you of how much I love and care about you. This gift does not come close to thanking you for your support and tolerance over these twenty-five years. I don't deserve you. You have always been there for me regardless of how inconsiderate I was. You have been my rock and my anchor. You are truly a great lady that I have been honored to call my wife. My darling, the bad stuff is all behind us. Let us spend the rest of our lives dedicated to each other. (She accepted the gift, hugged and cried in his arms." The pause brought tears to many an eye accompanied with loud approving applause.

After regaining his composure, he continued, "To my twelve children, I have not always been there for you but I will try to do better. I wish you all success and happiness and ask your forgiveness for my shortcomings. Mrs. Myrie and I have a present for each of you. I hope it will help you to realize your dreams." As was his style, he finished by reciting a poem by an unknown author:

"There comes a time in your life, when you walk away from all the drama and people who create it. You surround yourself with people who make you laugh. Forget the bad and focus on the good. Love the people who treat you right, pray for the ones who don't. Life is too short to be anything but happy."

I accept the fact that I have an appointment with the cemetery. For a long time, we worry about how to stay alive; then we spend the rest of our lives worrying about how not to die.

Life is like a roll of toilet paper, the closer you are to the end, the faster it spins. The longer I live, the fewer months there are in a year and the weeks go flying by. Recognizing that my life and yours cannot go on forever compels me to find meaning and happiness in every minute. But even though my eyes are dark and my spirits dimed, I still feel longevity in my bones. I hope both you and I will be around for a while longer. Thank you for coming. Good night." The applause was deafening.

Carolyn then came to the microphone with a standing ovation and vigorous hand clapping and shouts of praise from her possie (Shirley, Augustine, Patsy, Beulah and Rema), "What do you do if your husband is on the ground crying out in agony?" After a long pause, she continued, "Shoot him again!" (Roars of laughter) "There is also the story of a man on this death bed who felt a need to get things off his chest. He said, "Darling, I am dying and I ask your forgiveness. I have been unfaithful to you. I made love with four of your girl friends, your mother, the helper as well as at least one hundred other women. Please forgive me so I can go to my maker with a clean heart." The wife merely responded, "That's all right my darling, all is forgiven. Now, just relax and make the poison work." (Again, there was so much laughter. Tears flowed from many an eye)

Unlike the wives depicted in these stories, I bear no ill will for Mr. Myrie. In fact, I not only love him, I have the ultimate respect for a man who participated in the liberation of Angola and a highly successful businessman and politician. He continues to be a source of inspiration and a bright light in the lives of many families. My marriage has not always been a bed of roses, but I knew what I was getting into, and for the most part, he has been a good provider, a good partner and a good man. There is more joy in heaven over one sinner who repents than a crowd of goody goody people. According to Mr. Shakespeare:

"Let me not to the marriage of true minds
Admit impediments. Love is not love
Which alters when it alteration finds,
Or bends with the remover to remove:
O no; it is an ever-fixed mark,
That looks on tempests, and is never shaken;
It is the star to every wandering bark,
Whose worth's unknown, although his height be taken.
Love's not Time's fool, though rosy lips and cheeks
Within his bending sickle's compass come;
Love alters not with his brief hours and weeks,
But bears it out even to the edge of doom.
If this be error and upon me proved,
I never writ, nor no man ever loved."

My dear man, I will always love, respect, and cherish you. Our fates are entirely intertwined and our fortunes are one. Thank you for this beautiful watch and thank you for twenty five good years together. Let's go home and really celebrate!"

The applause was loud filling the room with laughter and shouts of "yea Mon!"

Defiant to the end, even with the disappointment and frustrations of his failing health, this humble peasant is determined to lose the "perturbations, noise and confusion" from his life. His wife and children took over the management of the business as he simplified his routines, consolidated his business interests and became a wonderful family man doting over his grandchildren with his wife by his side.

End of story. Full stop!

Mr. Garnett Myrie, Prime Minister of Jamaica, the Honorable Portia Simpson Miller, and Mrs. Carolyn Myrie at their twenty fifth wedding anniversary.

A Tribute to My Grandmother: Rosie McKenzie

Lessons Learned at My Granny's Knees

I served as the chief executive officer for the Association of Black Cardiologists (ABC) in Atlanta for twenty-one years, and I am generally known for having coined the tag line "Children Should Know Their Grandparents so they will become great-grandparents." This obviously related to my attempt to motivate people to develop healthy lifestyles so they will live long enough to help nurture their grandchildren as well as their great great grandchildren. It is a very special responsibility that I take more seriously now that I am a grandfather—six-times over. Until you have held a grandchild in your arms, you cannot imagine the joy! If I had known how much fun they were going to be, I would have had them first.

Except in Japan, there are never enough grandparents to positively impact on the ambitions of children. If we are ever going to solve our social problems (juvenile delinquency, unwanted pregnancies, unruliness and underachievement), we need the influence of grandparents and, preferably, great-grandparents. I am deliberate about advocating my seven steps to good health so our grandparents will leave later. You may have heard me expound on this theme on the "Tom Joyner Morning Show" and "All things Considered" (NPR). My professional and personal mission has been to stop the thief that is stealing our grandparents—heart disease.

I am sentimental about grandparents because I spent my impressionable years in the care of my fabulous Granny in Woodlands District. She will always be part of my soul. When I was twelve years old, if you had placed my mother and father in a police lineup, I could not have identified either one. My grandmother raised me and was the permanent fixture in my life. So I subscribe to the African proverb that advise us that when a grandparent dies, an entire library goes up in flames. She was a one of a kind and the library of my youth.

Having spent her entire life in St. Elizabeth, my grandmother (Rosie) was fifty nine years old when my mother placed my younger brother Earl who was three years old and me, a year older in her care and went off to 'merica. Granny died when she was seventy-six, leaving in her wake, fourteen children and a lifetime of generosity and good deeds. I believe that within every mango seed is the promise of a forest. Just imagine that the mango started out in Bombay, India, and it is now available worldwide. In a million years, my granny will have spawned millions of descendants. So far, she has forty grandchildren, twenty four great-grandchildren and sixteen great-great-grandchildren. Through it all, I always felt that "Granny" belonged only to me. I had endless unsettled arguments with numerous cousins (particularly Carlen McDonald) about whose Granny she was and convinced myself that she was "My Granny." While I was in college, a letter from me to her arrived the day she died affirming my gratitude and affection that was read at her funeral. Regretfully, it was impossible for me to attend. I will be forever indebted to her for her love and guidance. She actually believed that all children should be raised by their grandparents; "What do parents know about raising children?"

Mrs. Rosella McKenzie

I had the same sense of possessiveness when my first grandchild was born. After I was informed that my daughter (Jillian Kong-Sivert) had gone into labor, my wife, Stephanie, and I took a flight from Atlanta to Baltimore to camp out in the waiting room of the hospital to await the arrival of our precious little princess (Mackenzie). Unfortunately, in the same waiting room were my ex-wife and her new husband as well as my son-in-law's two sets of parents. While they all claimed to be grandparents to this child, I tried to convinced them that this was (in deed) my grandchild and invited them all (to no avail) to go home and not crowd up the place.

The same issue comes up annually when some of my four children do not show up for Thanksgiving or Christmas because they are also obligated to spend time with their in-laws. How unreasonable is that? Stephanie and I cannot seem to convince them that there are fifty other weeks when they are welcome to visit their in-laws with no protests from us. Are we the only ones that are reasonable and completely logical about this?

After my brother Earl and I moved in with our grandmother, she immediately enrolled us in Ms. Gatty's play school where we played, danced and sang songs all the livelong day in her yard.

Granny was always telling us that Woodlands is a healthiest place in the world to live. She pointed out to us that the support of family, neighbors and friends, the sunshine, cool breeze from our mountainside, clean rainwater, fresh air to breathe and all natural foods to eat with lots of opportunities to lively up ourselves are the ingredients of a good long life. At least once per day, children would hear, "Be pure, honest, sober, industrious, and considerate of others and success in life is assured." This became our mission in life.

To make her point, she told us the story of Brother Boogs who was born in Woodlands but was raised by a Chinese family (Old Chen and Ms. Ada), grew up with their sons Harry and Caz). At fifteen, he was sent off to Kingston to attend Kingston College. He suffered through his education because the city ginals always made fun of his country talk and dress. He became an Engineer and was never without work as employers preferred to hire people from St. Elizabeth because of our reputation for honesty and hard work. "When you say you are from St. Elizabeth, that's all the recommendation you need to get a job."

While Brother Boogs was only forty years old, however, he felt unsettled and lonely, lost his appetite along with all vim and vigor. He felt tired and his heart was empty. His weight was down to little or nothing. He never understood how Kingston people dress up so nice to attend church but their lives were devoid of honesty, integrity, caring or sympathy for others. He became depressed and sullen and stayed awake at night worrying about threats on his life by gangs, betrayal of his so-called friends and the general hostility of people he encountered. He became severely ill and nothing the doctors at Kingston Public Hospital prescribed on his frequent visits helped. In the parlance of Jamaica, "De man was sick, sick, sick, sick, sick, sick, sick, sick."

Believing that he was terminally ill, he left his employment and returned to Woodlands to die but failed. On his return, the Chinese family that raised him migrated, and he was able to reclaim the shop, house, and land that they left behind. His neighbors were so glad to see him back; they visited him regularly, carrying in their tureens, curry goat and rice, pumpkin soup with corn meal dumplings, roast yam, calaloo and salt fish, brown stew chicken, cane juice, custard apple and sour sap juice and best of all, corn pone and sweet potato pudding. The carrot juice with sweet milk and a Dragon Stout put lead back in his pencil. He developed a strong liking for "flumbadip" that was made from salt pork with coconut custard and red natta. Maybe there was something about food being the way to a man's heart as that was Ms. Dinah's specialty.

The minister heard he was on his deathbed, visited him accompanied by the choir and prayed over him as well as sing his favorite hymns. Brother Boogs was encouraged to visit the neighbors as well whenever he felt like it without even having to be invited or make an appointment. And when he visited, everyone made him feel special with lots of hugs and kisses. He recovered nicely. In three months, his appetite returned and he slept like a baby. He fell in love with Miss Dinah, a good cook and charming country girl who was a member of the church choir. She attended to his every need. They were regularly seen taking long walks and visiting family and friends with their arms around each other and sporting broad smiles.

He put some seeds in the soil and reopened the grocery shop that became a popular place to visit with friends. He also bought an automobile, joined the choir and taught Sunday School. He eventually got married and fathered two beautiful daughters (Izet and Sylvie, as well as a son (Francisco), who, along with his beautiful wife, were good reasons for living. Whenever he went to 'town' for supplies to stock the shop, he found time to recommend his therapy to all the business associates he encountered. For those who knew him as a depressed skeleton, they were amazed at his new lease on life.

It was not to last, however, as his sweet attentive wife died in childbirth along with their fourth child. After that, he no longer desired the company of any other woman, drank a great deal of rum and sang mournful songs but was known near and far as the best man to shoe horses and was also known to place large bets whenever there were horse races at New Pon. His daughters became nurses and went off to 'merica, built him a house and had him visit them in 'merica. But whenever he visited, after a few weeks he would be desperate to come back to Woodlands where he was as happy as he could be. He is remembered for devising the true test of friendship: play dead and see what your friends do.

My grandmother prayed unceasingly. God was a part of every sentence ("Lord willing, I will see you tomorrow"; "God bless you"; "Isn't God good?" What a friend we have in Jesus!). I have very vivid memories waking up early in the morning and seeing my grandmother on her knees beside her bed. She sang hymns such as "A Mighty Fortress is our God," "Rock of Ages," "My company before is gone and I am left alone with God," "brother, sister, let me serve you, let me be your servant too," "Amazing Grace" and her favorite: "Hark, the Voice of Jesus Calling:

Hark, the voice of Jesus calling,
"Who will go and work today?
Fields are white and harvests waiting,

Who will bear the sheaves away?"
Loud and long the master calls you;
Rich reward he offers free.
Who will answer, gladly saying,
"Here am I. Send me, send me"?

If you cannot speak like angels,
If you cannot preach like Paul,
You can tell the love of Jesus;
You can say he died for all.
If you cannot rouse the wicked
With the judgment's dread alarms,
You can lead the little children
To the Savior's waiting arms.

If you cannot be a watchman,
Standing high on Zion's wall,
Pointing out the path to heaven,
Offering life and peace to all,
With your prayers and with your bounties
You can do what God demands;
You can be life faithful Aaron,
Holding up the prophet's hands.

Let none hear you idly saying,
"There is nothing I can do,"
While the multitudes are dying
And the master calls for you.
Take the task he gives you gladly;
Let his work your pleasure be.
Answer quickly when he calls you,
"Here am I. Send me, send me!"

Author: Joseph Barnby (1869) Music: Daniel March, 1968

All day long while she cleaned the house, pick coffee, and prepare our meals the echo of her singing was ever present.

The reason I so enjoy the hugs and kisses of friends, family, and even strangers is that I could not leave her presence without a hug and kiss. I could not return from school without a hug and kiss. She would end each day sitting in her rocking chair reading her Bible for all to hear by the light of a kerosene lamp. My favorite place was sitting on the floor at her knees, with my back and head on her frock and apron while she stroked my hair.

She delighted in telling us Big Boy, Bra Nancy or duppy (ghosts) stories as well as tall tales and riddles. "Riddle me this and riddle me that, guess me this riddle and perhaps not. Sweet water standing." My favorite Bra Nancy Story was the time the best known Ginal in Jamaica went out to beg for food and came back with five bananas. Fortunately or unfortunately, he had a wife and four children. So he gave them each a banana and asked them not to worry about him as he did not mind going hungry. His wife immediately said she would not hear of it and gave him half of hers and the children followed suit resulting in them receiving a half each and Bra Nancy receiving two and a half. Big boy was asked if he knew who was crucified on the cross and didn't know the answer so the little girl behind him stuck him with a hat pin prompting him to yell, "Jesus Christ!" To which the teacher congratulated him for the right answer.

My imagination was active for days after some of her tall tales such as when a hunter ran out of lead bullets and used a seed to shoot an elephant. Years later when the hunter returned, he saw a large tree growing out of the elephant's head. With my granny, there was never a dull moment or a shortage of things to do (including Board games and Chinese checkers), except we were forbidden to play cards as she did not want to encourage gambling.

She always encouraged us to "do a ting" to make extra money. So in addition to raising rabbits and sowing carrot seeds and planting peas in land that I prepared myself, my brother and I made coconut drops and grater cakes and sold them at Mass Claudie's shop. We were able to double our money by investing in a coconut, a pound of sugar and a little ginger. With that profit margin, I could have made a quick million dollars by expanding my operations.

Nothing was more important to Granny than manners. Before we emptied the chamber pot at the root of the banana tree, we were obligated to say "Mawnin Granny" and say "Mawnin" with a smile to everyone we encountered on our way to school and generally speak to everyone. It was an absolute law in Granny's house that everyone greet each other on going to bed and rising. The law also extended to everyone we encountered on our way. It was culture shock to me that people in the United States could pass each other without saying something. "Please"; "Thank you, Ma'am"; "Good mawning"; and "Good night" were automatic. She smiled with pride when the neighbors told Granny how her half china pickney dem have manners. I found it strange when I migrated to 'merica and they said "Good evening" as a greeting instead of "Good night."

We never touched anything that didn't belong to us. Once when Aunt Myra was attending a function at church and asked me to run back to her house to retrieve something she forgot, she put some money on the bench beside me as a reward. Since she didn't say it belonged to me, I never touched it, and it became someone else's bounty. When we spent the night away from home, I always made the bed as soon as I got up. Don't touch your food until after the grace and until the person at the head of the table start eating.

Having observed several bright vibrant students from Woodlands win scholarship and go off to high school in Kingston only to return shell-shocked, depressed and withdrawn, Granny would caution students not to go off alone. She always felt like if there were at least two of them to support each other. They would be able to cope with the attacks of the Kingston Ginals who delighted in pointing out how country and backward the students were. Granny was told by one of the returning students that she was picked on from morning 'till night until she decided to forget about her education and come back to Woodlands just to keep her sanity. Once students went off to Kingston to go to school, they felt alienated from everyone they encountered, and if they stuck it out, they then felt alienated from Woodlands people because they had now adopted the ways of the city. They didn't feel like they belonged anywhere. In any case, Granny would advise the parents of these students to make sure there were at least two of them attending together. "Our children feel so loved here in Woodlands that they just cannot cope in the heartless city."

Growing up with Granny was a blessing. She was so noble in sentiment and entertaining in conversation. She could strategically place the right Bible passage in a conversation citing chapter and verse to make the point. She was everyone's friend and the neighbors treated her with love, respect and kindness. This poor country woman living in a very small unattractive frame house with four square rooms, scantily furnished and unadorned. It was a palace for all we knew. Granny invited confidences because she never betrayed a secret and was always sympathetic to the young women who sought her advice about their "man problems."

In reviewing our country lifestyle, I marvel that we ever got anything done other than tend to the necessities of living. In the city, they shopped for a week and store their food in refrigerators and pantries. In the country someone had to go to the shop to buy just enough for each meal. Water had to the fetched a mile away from the Parish tank. We would put a little branch from a tree to prevent the water from splashing as we carried the pan of water on our heads.

Someone also had to go a ground to dig up some yam, potatoes, badu or whatever was in season and find where the fowls had laid some eggs. On Sundays, it was my job to kill and pluck the chicken. I delighted in cutting off the head of the chicken and run after it for about a minute while it ran around like a chicken without its head. Then we also had to find wood for the fire, start fire (which was time-consuming). Even though we had to milk the cow, slop the pigs, throw corn to the chickens, plant, and weed the ground, pick pimento (all spice), coffee, cocoa, breadfruit, chocho and whatever fruits were in season, we found time for music, sports and visiting our neighbors. I made my own ping-pong table and paddles and we learned how to put the balls in hot water to round them out when they inevitably become dented.

Granny insisted that everything had to be clean and neat—a place for everything and everything in its place. We made up the bed and swept the floors every morning. Someone had to polish the reddish wooded floors each week. Our helper (Ms. Laurie) was very good at making music with the coconut brush and beeswax. I can still hear the rhythm. The other entertainment was listening to Miss Laurie wash our clothes. Sweet music man!

My granny was forever frustrated with people who only cared about themselves. Her favorite quote from the Bible was Philippians 2(4), "Let each of you look out not only for his own interests, but also for the interest of others." She also quoted Romans 14 (7), "For none of us live to himself alone and none of us dies to himself alone." "We shall all stand before the judgment seat of God." She often said, "So for what profit is it to a man if he gains the whole world, and loses his soul? (Mathew 16:26). This was her reason for being, her sermon, her cause and her message for all who would listen. At each evening meal, she made a plate for Mother Blake and another for Miss Poocus, single old ladies who had no one to care for them. I took one plate of food and my brother Earl took the other and returned with the plate from the day before. We would eat when we returned from our mission of mercy.

I was a very competitive boy. On numerous occasions, when I delighted in my own accomplishments, she was forever reminding me to never take pleasure only in my own success. When my learned aunt Madge (Allen) came home to visit for two weeks, she coached me about how to properly use my knife and folk as well as my arithmetic every day and I got all my sums right on the test. Granny wanted to know why we didn't help the others to do as well.

When we went to see a magic show at school, the family in front of us were in distress because they didn't have enough money. My granny conveniently pointed out to the mother that she must have dropped some of the money, which the children excitedly retrieved. When I became "Sports Champion" on Sports Day at Springfield School in 1958 by practicing in private, she wanted to know why I didn't help the other "Pickney dem" to do as well. She said to me, "I know you love to win and to succeed at things, but eventually, I hope you come to realize that helping others is even more fun." With my competitive proclivities at the time, she tried in vain to help me understand that, "If others succeed, you succeed; if they fail, you fail." Her criticism was, "Jamaicans are too selfish for our own good." She repeatedly preached to everyone that they should try to uplift those less fortunate, "Today for you, tomorrow for me." Or she would recall the words of Jesus, "As you did it to one of the least of these, my brethren, you did it to me. (Mathew 25:40)

On workday mornings, she boiled as opposed to brewed a big pot of coffee, extracted the bag of spent coffee grounds and added milk, sugar, and salt. She would then sit in her rocking chair with the pot beside her on the veranda. People on their way to work would stop for coffee, bring her a piece of yam, some bananas, a coconut, coco or dashine, enjoy a little conversation, and they were off again. She would invite them to come into the yard with, "Push the gate Mass Bertie." We never had a dog as she wanted nothing to impede or discourage visitors. One particular gentleman complained one morning that the coffee was not hot. The next morning, she heated the coffee, but the gentleman still complained that the coffee was not hot enough. Finally, she heated up the cup and the gentleman was happy. She would do anything to please. I hope the hot tin can didn't burn his lips.

During my entire childhood, I never met an evil person. No one ever meant to harm or stole from me. Obviously, we had school yard fights that my younger brother Earl would fight for me and any disagreement between neighbors would be referred to "Minister" or Justice Mair to fairly mediate and the disputing parties would shake hands and accept the settlement. There was a police station five miles away in New Market and maybe every six months a police officer would ride his horse up to the shop to have a "drink" with the men but I cannot remember anyone ever being arrested or ever had to go to court. Just seeing this police officer would strike terror in our hearts.

Other than using chew sticks, we did not know how to take care of our teeth so bad teeth was a problem as we ate sugar cane just about every day. As a temporary fix, Granny would soak a cotton ball in bay rum and place it on the offending tooth along with a cup of ganja or "collie weed" tea. One of my teeth was actually extracted by the shoemaker (Melvin Grey), as he was the only one with a pair of pliers. I suspect the toothbrush was invented in Woodlands by one of the old women with one tooth. If it had been invented anywhere else, it would have been called a teeth brush.

Here is a community activity I wish schools would readopt. Each morning, each student either brought some ground foods (yam, potato, dashine, coco, banana, corn, etc) or contribute a quatie (about three cents). The money was used to buy meat and flour to make dumplings. Everything was cooked up in a huge pot on an open wood fire by parents who volunteered. Come lunchtime, each student would receive a bowl of the stew with a soldier man (a one inch piece of meat) on top of the food. As we sat down together, no one could start eating before singing:

Be present at our table, Lord;
Be here and everywhere adored;
Thy creatures bless, and grant that we
May feast in paradise with Thee.
(Louis Bourgeois)

In addition to delicious but predictable menu at home, liver and light (lung) on Friday, soup (pumpkin, pepper pot, cowfoot, peas, or gungu) on Saturday, brown stew chicken with rice and peas (beans) on Sunday, I particularly liked smoked and roasted tripe (cow and pig intestines). The other delicious alternative was to pan fry some corn (salt) pork and pour all the grease over bread or breadfruit. I can still feel the grease in my palm from using my hand to wipe away the fat running down my chin as we never used napkins.

Bammy remains one of my favorite things to eat. We dug up the blue seal, cotton tree, black stick or white stick cassava roots, wash, peel and grater them. We then placed the slush into a straw basket that I would take up to Ms. Maude's house. The basket was placed on a flat stone with a bucket underneath to catch the juice, a wood plank was jammed into a tree root, ran on top of the basket and a large stone was tied to the end of the wooden plank pressing the juice out of the slush overnight. The next day, only the flour was left in the basket to be baked as bammy or boiled as cassava dumplings. When the juice settled, it produced starch and poison water. Interestingly enough, because the residue is high in cyanide, it was used to kill rats, mongoose and stray dogs. I cannot help wondering how much cyanide I have ingested over the years. The starch from our cassava was responsible for the stiff shirts and collars in Victorian England.

Woodlands specialized in growing yams of all kinds (yellow, white afro, St. Vincent, sweet, renta, pom-pom, yampi, macha, ghina, mozella, firefly, jackie, zippo, cobi, Trinidad, blue, and blue sprout). We enjoyed it boiled, baked, roasted, and even fried up with corn pork. Yams also contain cyanide.

Granny was also the doctor of the community if for no other reason that she preached "Cleanliness is next to Godliness" at every opportunity. I have no idea where she got a syringe but she used it to extract wax and corn bugs that occasionally became logged in people's ears while they slept. It was an agonizing experience until it floated out in the soapy water that Granny repeatedly sprayed into the ear. She often made a paste with "chick weed" and placed it on our wounds for quick healing. Like me, most country boys have machete cuts below their left knee and this was the cure for the "sore foot."

In a ritual she called our "wash out", she also wormed us twice per year. You do not want to know the details of this ritual of Sena tea and cod liver oil. I once pulled a foot-long tapeworm from my you know what.

In addition to hurricanes, Woodlands is also located on a fault line. We were sitting in our dining room in 1952 when the earthquake struck. While my brother and I were paralyzed with fear, Granny pushed back the cabinet that was about to fall, then she held onto the panya jar that was also falling. It was quite a sight. When the tremors stopped, while God had spared our house, we ran around the neighborhood evaluating the damage and found some houses ruined and that a big hole (fifty foot wide) had opened up and swallowed a dozen trees about ten chains from our house.

As we are protected from high winds by the mountains around us, we did not have devastating hurricanes and we would enjoy running around picking up avocado pears, coconuts, oranges or whatever fell from the trees. Everyone had a mackerel barrel full of fruits that were prematurely blown off the trees. When I was ten years old, a hurricane named "David" devastated Jamaica and met another hurricane named "Florence" who was leaving Cuba headed for Jamaica. Florence asked David how it was in Jamaica and David told Florence that the politicians had already mashed up Jamaica, so she veered off to Mexico.

As my mother sent us a lot of balls and toys, there was never a shortage of children in our yard. We also had a lot of land available for cricket, football and catch me games. For the cricket bat, we used a coconut bough. When I was fourteen, my Uncle Ronnie migrated to England and left me his bicycle. I sold rides on my bicycle for a penny until someone slammed it into a tree and put an end to my little enterprise and my own transportation. It was never repaired. My slingshot was always in my back pocket, and there were always smooth small stones in my side pocket just in case we encountered a bird. A lady came to our school one day to ask us not to shoot the beautiful song birds but I don't recall that her speech curtailed our hunting. We roasted the naked birds on hot coals and ate them while licking our fingers.

Granny could never stop smiling when mangoes came in. She would say; "A good mango season is a reminder of how much God loves us." We would bring home basketful after basketful and we would all sit around the basket and polish off those beautiful sweet mangoes that left the creamy juice dripping down our chins and turn the front of our shirts and blouses a bright orange and left stings in our teeth. What's for dinner Granny? "I turned over the cook pot. It's mango season." It was really, really special when she served ice cream with slices of mango.

It made sense to her that night air was dangerous. She had observed that people who stayed out late at night often got sick and even died. So as soon as it got dark, she closed all the windows, stuck pieces of cloth in the holes and would not allow us to go outside. All her chickens had to be indoors. This puzzled me for years until I had an aha moment fifty years later and realized that she had good reason to came to this conclusion from her experience during a malaria (dhengue) outbreak. As mosquitoes came out at dusk, people who stayed out at night were more likely to be bitten by these pests that carried the malaria parasite, got sick, and even died. Interestingly enough, I happened to be reading The Lives of Celebrated Travelers by James Augustus St. John and published by Harper and Brothers (NY) in 1854 and came across this passage, "In observing on the thirty-first of July an eclipse of the moon, he imprudently exposed himself to the night dew, and next day, he found himself attacked by fever and delirium, which were the commencement of an illness that with very trifling intermission confined him during two months within doors." This myth has been around for a long time. I have a feeling it was malaria. I suspect is was the British who spread the myth aroud the world that consumption was caused by exposure to fowl weather or a draft.

When I was about ten years old, Granny became concerned about duppies causing mischief on our zinc roof at night. She asked the local Obeahman to come, and he prescribed the burning of sulfur candles at night. When she followed his advice, the house smelled so putrid, we had to run outside and stayed there (night air or no night air) for several hours until the smell dissipated. I suspect, the noises were rats or even bats. The Obeahman, on the other hand, was useful to prepare the cricket pitch when we had a game with a visiting team. Chanting a few songs and sprinkling fresh chicken blood would absolutely guarantee a victory.

Granny taught us the recipe for rum punch:

One of sour (lime juice)
Two of sweet (strawberry syrup)
Three of strong (Over proof white rum)
Four of weak (water)
A dash of angostura bitters, and you are good to go.

The hurricane pattern for Jamaica was also put to poetry:

June too soon
July stand by
August you must
September remember
October all over.

My granny was also a genius of recycling as she heartily subscribed to the old Jamaican adage, "What no dead no dashway." Solder a handle on a condensed milk can and you have a coffee mug. Chicken Feed bags made shirts. Glue could be made from pouring kerosene on anything made from rubber. To this day, my wife will attest that like all Jamaicans, I have a hard time throwing things out. More importantly, I hate waste, especially time. I want to fill every minute with sixty seconds of useful activity. "If you waste time, time will waste you." I would actually go mad if I did not have books available at all times. When I reflect on how much knowledge and joy I have received from the thousand or so books I have read, I lament with great guilt that one third of the people of Jamaica have never read a book.

It is a little unbelievable that we generated no garbage. Leftover food was fed to the pigs including banana and breadfruits peels that we boiled in old kerosene tins. Any paper and particularly newspaper we received from buying salt fish, flour, sugar, salt, and bread ended up beside the toilet to be read just prior to its final disposal. Bottles were valuable to store cooking oil, carry water, to make a firelight when traveling at night or returned to the shop for a refund. A broken plate was made into small disks with the decoration on one side and white on the other that we would throw to the ground with the winner being whoever had the most flowers. We had no plastic. Even at the shop, we merely washed the glasses in the soap basin, rinse them and turn them upside down on pegs. When we took baths, the remaining bath water was used to hydrate trees. Nothing was wasted.

There is a familiar Jamaican proverb that advises that one can "tun han and mak fashion." The essence of the thought is that you can work with what you have, however modest it may be. Granny was always fixing things as well as make things stretch. When a hole appeared in the cook pot, she used a hammer to ram some cloth into the space and continued to cook with it. She was always darning socks by placing an egg inside the worn area and pull thread through each edge. We made our own hula hoops from a bicycle tire and when it wasn't a hula hoop, we bent a wire around it and pushed it around as if we were driving an automobile. We even made our own marbles from clothes wire and sand paper stones until they were round. Did I mention that we also made the sand paper? We fashioned gigs from guava limbs as well as sling shots from a wishbone limb, a small piece of leather and some rubber from a bicycle tube.

My most indelible memory, however, related to the brutal lashing I received at the hands of our headmaster when I was twelve years old. Thursday afternoons were to be spent working in the garden (model farm) to teach us to be good cultivators. All of us hated the back breaking work in the hot sun including the teachers who were supposed to be supervising us but were often elsewhere having tea. We also resented the fact that all the food from this garden ended up in teacher's kitchen. Well, four of us boys went off to play cushou (marbles). In Woodlands, we call it chushu. Just when I said "rounds two" and took aim with my marble at the pile of cashews in the circle we had marked out on the ground, Screw face Teacher Harry Crawford jumped over the wall and ran toward us. We were paralyzed with fear and resisted the temptation to run. He went from one boy to the next and angrily beat us with a guava switch. When I went home, the blood from the welts on my back had caked on my shirt. Ordinarily Granny took up for the teacher but this was too much. He had crossed the line.

Granny marched me up to the headmaster's cottage and stood at Teacher Crawford's gate and cussed him for about an hour. This is the one and only time she ever lost her cool. She was fit to be tied. She marched back and forth in front of his gate and yelled obscenities at him and called him every awful name that she could think of in front of the crowd that had gathered. I was feeling sorry for teacher. She characterized him as a monster for brutalizing her child. With that performance, I could no longer return to school. So she took me to Nightingale Grove School (three miles away) and boarded me with Headmaster Marvin Morris during the week. My academic performance accelerated during that year with the help of another student (Lizette Sherman) who was also boarding with Teacher Marvin Morris and I felt very big up walking to school with the headmaster each morning.

A year later, Teacher Crawford was replaced by the very talented and superb teacher Clifford Chang and his wife Joyce. I returned to Springfield School to enjoy my final year in Jamaica with my granny—my inspiration, mentor, and the best teacher to whom I owe my broughtupsy.

Yes. Everyone loved Ms. Rosie. She was kindness incarnate. In fact, if you look up the word "kindness" in Webter's Dictionary, you will find her picture. Who would not love someone who was always ready to lend a helping hand and to offer whatever she had to improve the human condition. I have never met anyone who was more generous and who had the uncanny ability to lift the spirits of all who came in contact with her. She taught me that the more she gave away, the more she got in return, and it was always better to give than to receive. Her direct words were, "Good deeds are like seeds planted in rich soil, guaranteed to return a good harvest."

Soon after I migrated to the United States, I obtained a job as a dishwasher in the Spring Garden restaurant in Morristown, New Jersey. My granny would get a taste from my first pay and would continue to receive a share from all my future income until she died.

Now, before you start claiming her as your granny. Don't forget that she is mine. Interestingly enough, there are many other grannies like Ms. Rosie around Woodlands—even today!

GLOSSARY

1. "U a bawn ya": Born in Jamaica

2. "One a wi": one of us Jamaican patois does not use "us" but "we" pronounced "wi"

3. "Wata come a mi eye": When I cried

4. "buck upon": Accidentally met

5. "tun han make fashion": Apply ingenuity to use whatever you may have even if they are scraps to make fashionable clothes. Better yet, become like a Phoenix rising from the ashes to achieve greatness. It is a marvel to see families emerging from shacks on Sunday mornings, clean, every hair in place, shoes shined, wearing pretty dresses and dark suits on their walk to the altar.

6. "Bid Whist": A card game similar to bridge but more vigorously played

7. "Wa mi fi do?": What can I do?

8. "Dog nam yu supper": It is unfortunate and I am sorry, but there is nothing to be done.

9. The National Anthem of England

10. The National Anthem of Jamaica

11. "Manley era migration": Many wealthy Jamaicans detested the policies of Prime Minister Michael Manley, the fourth prime minister of Jamaica who served from 1972-1980. He was a Robin Hood politician who taxed the rich to improve the lot of the poor. When the rich protested, he said, "There are three flights per day to Miami. If you don't like what we are doing in Jamaica, pack your bags and go." Many rich Jamaicans left with their funds, knowledge, and skills creating a dramatic fall in real estate value, unemployment, and a shortage in skilled manpower. He is credited, nevertheless, for uplifting the plight of the poor.

12. "Ginals": Con artists but lovable con artists

13. "Calaloo": Jamaican spinage

14. "town": Kingston

15. "Been to houses": Jamaicans who went abroad (foreign) and return with wealth to build large houses.

16. "Barber-Greene": The name on the equipment that made asphalt roads. The company was founded by Harry Barber and William Greene. The name was adopted to describe the resulting paved road. Some of these roads also had streets lights that the people called, "Moon pon stick."

17. "Yard" or "Rock" designates "Jamaica": A "Yardie" is a Jamaican.

18. "Cotching": Getting by on the good will of others as in sleeping on someone's couch.

19. "Daya": Here, where I am. "I am just hanging out here."

20. "Tastee or Juici": The main two brands of patty shops in Jamaica.

21. "Cooshues": A popular restaurant in Mandeville fashioned from an old bus.

22. "Hellshire Beach": A popular beach town twenty miles from Kingston that is famous for fried fish and festival (fried dumplings).

23. "Devon House": An incredibly beautiful 127-year-old house on 11 acres in Kingston that was built by a black Jamaican millionaire (George Stiebel). He was greatly resented by the establishment for his success. It now operates as a national monument with upscale restaurants and shops. The very best ice cream is Jamaica or anywhere is Devon House Ice Cream.

24. "Sabina Park": The cricket stadium in Kingston

25. Gleaner: The oldest and most prestigious newspaper in Jamaica operating since 1834. It was started by Joshua and Jacob De Cordova.

26. "Sorrell": A Red Christmas drink often mixed with ginger and rum. It is made from hibiscus. It is also called the fleur de Jamaica, Zombo, and Roselle. It is now readily available in Jamaica throughout the year.

27. "Father Christmas": Santa Claus

28. "Broughupsy": How one was raised

29. "strapin": Stronger and more robust

30. "crocus bags": Bags used to transport sugar, flour, etc.

31. "Hunk": A large piece of something good like hard dough bread or Easter bun.

32. "Dutch pot": All our pots were imported from the Netherlands. You may remember the words to the song "Pass the Duthie on the right hand side."

33. "Tilley lamp": A popular English-made hydropneumatic kerosene lamp sold throughout the English Empire.

34. "paradise plums": A sour citrus candy otherwise called "sweetie."

35. "Bulla": A large soft cookie made from flour, molasses, and sugar.

36. "didn't break an egg": Scored zero

37. "China nam dog": A derogatory curse directed at Chinese people who were accused of eating dogs. What one eats in Jamaica is a great source of rejection. Things that could not be eaten include mushrooms.

38. "Farrin": Overseas, anywhere that is not Jamaica

39. "Clide": To be sick and tired of eating the same thing over and over

40. "aerated wata": A soft drink, soda water, coke, etc.

41. "Champaign cola": A popular orange flavored softdrink

42. cerese tea: A popular and bitter herb that is said to cure any number of ailments as well as lighten the skin of babies, born, and unborn.

43. "provision ground": Typically, these are about an acre of land (enough for one man to cultivate), part of the land dedicated to yams, part to carrots, part to "red peas" (beans), coco, dashine, and badu. Jamaican farmers do not specialize in one crop but combine their crops—a little piece of this and a little piece of that.

44. "liad": A liar

45. "facey": Fresh, too big for his britches

46. "Go whey": Go away. I want nothing more to do with you.

47. "yuths": Children

48. "Catta": A cushion of leaves or cloth between the load and their heads which also helps to balance the load so they can walk without holding on to whatever they were carrying.

49. "panya jar with a thunder ball": A Spanish-styled clay jar where a smooth stone was placed to keep the drinking water cool.

50. "Kin puppu lick": Do summersaults

51. "Full stop": The period at the end of a sentence or the end of a strong point

52. The song "LONG TIME GAL" captures the job of Jamaican life

This long time gal me never see yuh (I haven't seen you in a long time)
Come mek me hold yuh hand (Let me hold your hand)

This long time gal me never see yuh
Come mek me hold yuh hand
Peel head John Crow sit upon the tree top (Look around you. Do you see the buzzard?)
Pick out the blossom (and all the flowers around you?)
Mek mi hold yuh han Gal
Mek mi hold yuh hand

Long time gal me never see yuh
Come mek we walk and talk (Let's take a walk and have a long talk)
Long time gal me never see yuh
Come mek we walk and talk
Peel head John Crow sit upon the tree top
Pick out the blossom
Mek mi walk and talk Gal
Mek mi walk and talk Gal

Long time gal me never see yuh
Come mek we wheel and Jig (I am in such a happy mood, let's dance)
Long time gal me never see yuh
Come mek we wheel and Jig (turn me round and dance)

Peel head John Crow sit upon the tree top
Pick out the blossom
Mek mi hold wheel and Jig Gal
Mek mi hold wheel and Jig
Mek mi hold yuh hand
Mek mi hold wheel and Jig Gal
Mek mi walk and talk Gal

53. "Pukkumania": A local religion characterized by spirited drumming, singing, dancing, spirit-possession, speaking in tongues, and healing rituals.

54. "Bammy": Bread made from cassava flour

55. "Anancy": A cunning spider character in Jamaican stories who always prevail against great odds.

56. "Feefees": A toy that rolled out like a striking snake with a hissing sound when blown into and curls up again when the air is exhausted. It is repeated to the delight of the children.

57. "Cumback": Bread and butter

58. "Force ripe": Rather than let things take their course naturally, use tricks to hasten the ripening of fruit. This can be dangerous if you force ripe ackee. "Force ripe man": When boys grow up fast, having to take responsibility for the family with the passing of parents, having sexual experiences too early, etc.

59. "Jankonoo": A street parade with music and dancing but the focus is on the masks.

60. "Bush tea": Teas are very popular in Jamaica and can be brewed from a thousand different sources from orange leaves, ganja and willow bark.

61. "Jucked": To poke someone in the side with a finger

62. "egg red": The yolk of an egg

63. "the eye of an egg": The germinal cell

64. "Boosey": A dressed up man who feels very prideful

65. "Mi no wa fi do it": I don't want to do it

66. "Bus-mi-jaw-bone": A very hard molasses and coconut candy capable of breaking jaws if not eaten carefully

67. "Gizadas": A small pie with coconut and sugar filling

68. "Love weed": A bright red stringy parasite plant that grows on the sides of roads. It is a true test of whether someone love you if you pick some of it, throw it over your shoulder and yell the person's name out loud.

69. "Licking the challace": Smoking a ganja pipe

70. "Groundings": Dr. Rodney referred to his street meetings as groundings as in getting down to the basics.

71. "Heavy manners": Frequently keeping one's foot on someone else's throat.

72. "Fire bun. Idiot thing dis": Let's burn the damn place down. It cannot get any worse.

73. "Every man jack": Everyone, the entire community

Important Dates

AD 600:	Yamaye (Jamaica) inhabited by Tainos/Arawacks
May 5, 1494:	Columbus arrives and declares Jamaica a a Spanish conquest
1500:	Bachelor Gonzalo de Velosa made sugar from sugar cane
1517:	Spain imported slaves to Jamaica
1655:	England took Jamaica from the Spaniards and established colonial rule
1661:	English decreed that children born out of wedlock could not inherit from their father
1692:	Port Royal Earthquake
1923:	Founding of the Poetry League of Jamaica
1834:	After authorizing slavery in the commonwealth for 300 years, the Act of Emancipation freeing all slaves in the Empire was passed in England
1938:	The Launch of the PNP Party (Norman Manley)
March 23, 1942:	Dr. Rodney's birth in Guyana
1943:	The Launch of the JLP (Alexander Bustamante) First free elections in Jamica
August 17, 1951:	Hurricane Charlie
1951:	Bauxite is discovered in Jamaica
September 27, 1953:	The birth of Garnett Myrie
1955:	The first Staging of the Jamaica National Festival

1955:	Rosa Parks refused to take her seat at the back of the bus in Birmingham, AL
1955-1975:	US/Vietnam war
1957:	Southern Christian Leadership Council (SCLC) is formed in Atlanta
1957-1967:	The great migration of skilled Jamaicans to England
1959:	The National Stadium is built under the administration of Michael Manley
1961:	Stokely Carmichael popularize "Black Power"
1962:	Jamaica became a semi-independent nation with a Governor General.
1962-'67:	Prime Minister Alexander Bustamante's term of office (JLP)
1963:	Ms. Carolyn Crawford (Jamaican) was crowned "Miss World"
October 5-7, 1963:	Hurricane Flora
November 15, 1963:	Marcus Garvey Enshrined in Jamaica
April 21, 1965:	Dr. Martin Luther King delivers speech at The University of the West Indies. (Even though political leaders in thought of him as a threat, Professor Anthony Allen was honored to host him.)
1965:	The Voting Rights Act signed into law in the United States
1966:	His Majesty Haile Selassie I visits Jamaica
1967-1972:	Prime Minister Hugh Shearer's term of office (JLP)

October 14, 1968:	Dr. Rodney expelled from Jamaica
1969:	Tommi Smith and John Carlos gave the black power salute at the Olympic Games
1968:	The Civil Rights Act became law
October 14, 1968:	Garnett Myrie migrates to Cuba
September 2, 1969:	Death of Honourable Norman Manley (PNP)
February 23, 1970:	Sir Donald Sangster becomes the second prime minister only to die in office three months later on April 11.
1972-'80/'89-'92:	Prime Minister Michael Manley's terms of office (PNP)
1973:	Free Education up to high school comes to Jamaica
October 18, 1977:	Fidel Castro visits Jamaica
August 4-7, 1980:	Hurricane Allen
1980-1989:	Prime Minister Edward Seaga's term of office (JLP)
1987 (September, 11):	Peter Tosh is shot to death in his home by intruders
September 12, 1988:	Hurricane Gilbert
1992:	The film:"Malcolm X" is released
1994-2006:	Prime Minister P. J. Paterson's term of office (PNP)
September 10-11, 2004:	Hurricane Ivan
August 2007:	Hurricane Dean
November 2008:	Barack Hussein Obama II elected president of the United States
2006-2007/2012:	Prime Minister Portia Simpson Miller's terms of office

INDEX

soldiers, 19, 77, 81, 105, 143, 145, 147, 194

songs, 37, 54, 80, 87, 133, 163, 198, 206-7

soul, 21, 45, 53, 115, 162, 164-66, 182, 191

South Africans, 143, 146

Southern Christian Leadership Council (SCLC), 212

Spanish Needle, 60, 100

Sports Day, 102, 104, 192

Springfield, 18, 22-23, 26, 31, 34, 42, 44, 49, 51, 67, 192, 200

stealing, 41, 74-75, 88, 93, 117-18, 123, 139, 152, 182

St. Elizabeth, 7, 13, 28, 49, 108, 133, 176, 182, 184

Stephanie, 7, 183-84

stories, 8-9, 13, 19, 24, 28, 36, 50, 63, 78, 98, 129, 134, 136, 140, 153, 178, 180, 184, 188

students, 36, 89, 96, 102, 125, 190, 194, 200

sugar, 38, 40, 43, 97, 192, 199, 206, 210-11

wet, 38, 67, 77

Sundays, 25, 38, 87-88, 191, 194

Sunday school, 50, 60, 84, 86, 186

superego, 118-20

T

taxes, 170, 172-73

Teacher Crawford, 200

Teacher Ferguson, 71-72, 76

teachers, 16, 50, 60, 65, 71-74, 89-90, 92, 94, 96, 102, 105,

107, 125, 144, 188, 199-200

testimonials, 161, 165, 175

Tosh, Peter, 121-22, 127, 133, 156, 177, 213

toys, 14-15, 26, 62, 196, 209

trees, 24-25, 31, 38, 43, 56, 77, 79, 137, 142, 146, 166, 191, 196

mango, 78, 110, 138, 146

U

Uncle Claudie, 40-45

underground economy, 171-72

United States, 9, 14, 17-18, 20, 24-25, 28, 36, 47, 90, 115-16, 143-44, 156, 174, 189, 201, 212-13

universities, 20, 115-16, 123, 125, 127, 152, 212

V

victims, 63, 95, 111, 114, 123-24, 171, 176

Viking Gang, 112, 123-24, 126

violence, 85, 111-12, 117, 125-26, 172

W

water, 7, 15, 21, 29, 31, 37, 41, 43, 54-56, 58, 62, 72, 74, 79, 81, 93, 96, 110, 146-47, 168-69, 190-91, 198-99

West Indies, 115-16, 125, 152, 212

wives, 7-8, 20, 23, 25, 31, 43, 49,

Edwards Brothers Malloy
Thorofare, NJ USA
May 27, 2014